To Elizabeth

May you enjoy

this touch of the South

in your Kitchen.

Love,

Mom

1997

MAGNOLIAS SOUTHERN CUISINE

SOUTHERN CUISINE

By

Donald Barickman

Photographs By Tom Eckerle
Project Consultant Marion Sullivan

Wyrick & Company

Published by Wyrick & Company
1–A Pinckney Street
Charleston, S.C. 29401

Manufactured in Hong Kong

Library of Congress Cataloging-in-Publication Data

Barickman, Donald, 1962–
Magnolias Southern cuisine / by Donald Barickman ; photographs by
Tom Eckerle ; project consultant Marion Sullivan.
p. cm.
Includes index.
ISBN 0-941711-31-5
1. Cookery American--Southern style. I. Title.
TX715.2.S68B37 1995
641.5975--dc20   95-12066
CIP

CONTENTS

This book is dedicated to our loyal local customers
for their year-round patronage, kind referrals
and for challenging us to continue to grow.

ACKNOWLEDGEMENTS

Thank you to my parents, Joyce and Woody Barickman, for patience, persistence and my Culinary Institute of America education.

To my wife Jennifer for her love, support and understanding of the endless tasks of my position, and for her devotion to the commitment of raising our twin sons, William and Stuart. I also include my thanks to Jennifer's parents Nancy and Norman Smith for their monumental endurance, both with me and our children. My special thanks to Nancy for her sense of the Southern palate which has helped me to better understand our cuisine.

Tom Parsell for the partnership that made Magnolias a reality, for the freedom to create its structure and cuisine, and for his administration of the business and marketing aspects of our growing company. I am also very grateful to Suzi Parsell for her unwavering support.

All of the Hospitality Management Group employees for their continuous hard work, their loyalty and their constant desire to maintain our high standards.

Especially to the very talented group of chefs who man our kitchens every day: Casey Taylor, Don Drake, Gerald Mitchell, Mike Dragon, Glynn Swain and Frank Strauss.

And to our baking team, headed by Pastry Chef Norma Naparlo.

Our purveyors for giving us the quality goods needed to make fine food.

My fellow Charleston chefs for their friendship and inspiration. Sharing the same marketplace has helped us to define the quality of the cuisine which has put Charleston on the map as a culinary destination.

Franz Meier for his confidence in giving me an Executive Chef position at the age of 24 and starting my training in the discipline of kitchen management.

Marion Sullivan for her knowledge and expertise in cookbook development.

Tom Eckerle for his masterful photographs and for the professionalism which makes working with him such a pleasure.

Pete Wyrick for making ours his first cookbook publication.

And last, but not least, my native West Virginians who frequently visit Magnolias to say hello and satisfy their curious appetites.

INTRODUCTION

Throughout this book, I make numerous references to the love of food that began in my childhood. Much of this I attribute to my parents and to the time that I spent in my grandparents' garden and kitchen. Simple food and good friends proved to be the rewarding and satisfying combination which led me into the hospitality industry.

In 1980, I started college in my home state at the West Virginia University. It was not long before it became clear that this was not where I was going to find a career. When I began a stint as a prep cook in the restaurant of a family friend, the light dawned. As I moved to other positions in the kitchen, I became fascinated with the various aspects of food production, and began to view this business as a true career opportunity.

With this in mind, I applied for study at The Culinary Institute of America in New York. I further prepared for school by helping a friend open a soup and sandwich deli. School started in the fall of 1983. While the first few days were somewhat intimidating, I soon found that I couldn't wait to get out of bed in the morning to attend class. It was our final class, however, that proved to be the most interesting to me. It involved working in the school's newly formed American Bounty Restaurant. After having studied most of the world's important cuisines, it was American food which seemed to provide the best opportunity for me to express what I wanted with my cooking.

My graduation goal became to seek out a small but challenging property which offered creativity, individuality, a close working relationship with talented chefs, and the availability of first-rate local products. I favored the South because my family had visited there frequently and I had become fond of the Southern coast. I chose Wild Dunes, a resort just north of Charleston which offered food service that ranged from fine dining to beach cookouts. I found the Charleston area to supply top quality fresh seafood and the surrounding Sea Islands to be bountiful in produce. It was in this year that I first began to understand the importance of using local products and supporting local purveyors and farmers. I enjoyed working with Chef Frank Lee. He was very focused and determined, but also knew how to inject a bit of humor when it was most appreciated.

My following year was spent as Sous Chef at The Wine Cellar, a 45-seat fine dining restaurant in downtown Charleston owned by M. & W. Associates. Soon, Franz Meier of M. & W. offered me the chef's position at their newest operation, Carolina's. The menu was to focus on Southern food and local ingredients, a perfect format for my interests. Carolina's was an immediate success. It was here that I was fortunate enough to begin to build the team of chefs who became not only good friends, but many of whom are key employees today at Magnolias. I give them credit for much of the success which I have enjoyed over the years.

Because of the success of Carolina's, M. & W. Associates planned to open a similar concept in the nearby capitol city of Columbia, and I was asked to open it with them. Columbia's, a 230-seat lunch and dinner establishment, opened in March of 1989, again to much success.

But it was coming back to Charleston that was the climax of all that I had worked for. I had been contacted by a well-known Charleston businessman, Thomas Parsell, who had purchased a building in the heart of Charleston's historic district shortly after hurricane Hugo. His idea was to turn this empty building into a restaurant. Tom had frequented Carolina's, was familiar with my cooking style, and complimented me by offering to establish Hospitality Management Group, Inc., with he and I as the principals.

This was my first opportunity to help develop the entire concept of a restaurant, design my own kitchen and train my own staff using the ideas that I had acquired through the years of working for others. I needed to build a kitchen which would effectively handle the volume that we had projected, yet make the job as easy as possible from a production standpoint. As time progressed and the facility took shape, I began to create the menu. We designed an extensive, all-day menu to offer appetizers, lunch items and entrées, serving from 11:00 A.M. until midnight. I had been experimenting with grits, the almost forgotten staple of the South, and planned to re-introduce them on the menu. Our grits dishes were to become some of our most popular signature items.

We decided on the name Magnolias Uptown/Down South to reflect our emphasis on Southern cuisine. After eight months of renovation and new construction, we opened the doors on the evening of July 31, 1990. It was a good thing that we were ready! We were immediately faced with some of the strongest business that I had ever seen.

After a highly successful two years of business, Tom Parsell realized that we had a continual problem: every week Magnolias was fully booked for the upcoming weekend by the preceding Tuesday or Wednesday, with most of our week nights being full as well. He was quick to react when a building next door became available. The property was purchased and we were back to the drawing board to conceptualize a whole new project. Our challenge was to create a concept that our clientele would enjoy which was totally different from Magnolias'. The answer was innovative American cuisine, drawing its influence from the Mediteranean and featuring fresh, regional ingredients. I was self-trained in pizzas years ago and was intrigued by the Italian made wood-burning pizza oven which we made the main focal point of our exhibition kitchen. The pastas and breads would be made fresh on a daily basis in our in-house bakery. The name: a bit of a spin-off, The Blossom Cafe. The Blossom kitchen staff was a simple transition of key kitchen employees from Magnolias who were eager to assume responsibilities and assert leadership. Working with Glynn Swain, Frank Strauss and Norma Naparlo as Pastry Chef, we gave the Cafe its groove of creativity and consistency, and satisfied many patrons with an exciting Magnolias alternative.

So it has been a rewarding journey from picking produce in my grandparents' garden and cooking pizzas on a stone in my mother's oven. But many things are still the same. Hospitality is still about good food and good people. We never forget that it is our customers and, primarily, our loyal local clientele to whom we owe our success. It is always our constant challenge to give them what they want. And that is precisely the motivation for publishing this cookbook. We have supplied an uncountable number of recipes over the years to satisfy the requests of our guests. It was time to finally present these recipes in an organized and orderly format. They have been converted from my kitchen environment to yours, and I think you'll find the procedures quite simple to follow. I hope that you enjoy the book.

Donald M. Barickman
Chef/Partner
Magnolias Uptown/Down South
Blossom Cafe

STARTERS

UPTOWN/DOWN SOUTH STARTERS

At Magnolias, we have created a selection of starters which gives our customers a light-hearted tour of our cuisine, from Bar-B-Que with Corn Bread Styx to Black-Eyed Pea Cakes with Red and Yellow Tomato Salsa to Pan-Fried Chicken Livers with Caramelized Onions, Country Ham and Red-Eye Gravy. Here's where you'll find our Sweet Pepper Relish, Bread and Butter Pickles and Peach Chutney. Try the Bar-B-Que in the Yellow Corn Biscuits or use the Pimiento Cheese as an hors d'oeuvre to spread on crackers or the Herb Toasts.

When you make our Parmesan Oysters or Down South Egg Rolls, remember that a healthy respect for the rules of frying will prevent unfortunate mistakes. Never put a pot full of oil on the stove and turn the heat up to high; always heat it up gradually. A simple candy thermometer will allow you to monitor the temperature of the oil. Keep in mind that adding the oysters, egg rolls or any fried item will raise the level of the hot oil. An overflow is a very easy way to start a grease fire. And finally: never leave anything that is frying unattended.

The breads in this chapter are integral parts of our Starter recipes. When you read our corn bread recipes, you'll see that I feel that the crust that you achieve by baking corn bread in a cast iron skillet is reason enough for owning what some would consider to be a historic relic. It's important to understand how to take care of your cast iron cookware. I think perhaps that's what puts most people off, even though it's so easy. A well seasoned cast iron pan is one that has all of its porous metal holes saturated or filled with oil through cooking. A new pan should be seasoned in the following manner:

- Preheat oven to 225 degrees.
- Wash the pan with hot soapy water, rinse and dry well.
- Fill the pan one-half of the way up with vegetable oil. This will saturate the pores as it is baking in the oven.
- Place the pan in the 225 degree oven for an hour.
- Remove the pan from the oven and let the oil cool. Pour the cooled oil back into its original container to dispose of it.
- Wipe the pan with a dry, clean towel.

Once a pan is seasoned in this manner, you'll want to take care of its finish. After cooking in a cast iron pan, it can be lightly scrubbed with hot soapy water and dried immediately. Do not leave the pan soaking in a sink of water or sitting wet on the counter. Cast iron will rust if not treated properly. Additionally, soaking will release all of the oil from the pan's porous metal holes and cause food to stick to the pan. After being dried, the pan should be given a light rub with oil before putting it away. When you bake Magnolias' Country Corn Bread in a seasoned cast iron skillet, I think you'll be convinced that using cast iron is worth the effort.

SPICY BLACK BEAN CAKES

Makes 20 2-ounce cakes

3 cups dried black beans

12 cups water

6 chicken bouillon cubes

1 teaspoon salt

2 smoked pork neck bones

2 Tablespoons olive oil

1/2 cup minced yellow onion

2 Tablespoons minced garlic

1/2 cup minced green onions

1/2 cup minced red onion

1/4 cup minced red pepper

1 Tablespoon stemmed, seeded
   and chopped jalapeño pepper

2 Tablespoons chopped cilantro

1 Tablespoon cumin

dash of cayenne pepper

2 teaspoons salt

1 teaspoon freshly ground black
   pepper

2 cups corn bread crumbs from
   Corn Bread recipe (see p. 30)

1 cup olive oil for frying

2 cups stone ground yellow
   cornmeal for dusting the cakes

Measure the black beans and pour them out onto a baking sheet. Pick through them and remove small pebbles and discolored beans. Put the remaining beans in a colander and rinse.

Using a large, heavy-bottomed saucepan, combine the beans, water, chicken bouillon cubes, salt and smoked neck bones. Bring to a boil.

Reduce to a simmer and cook for 2 to 2 1/2 hours or until the beans are very soft and their skins have broken. Add additional water if needed, a cup at a time. Remove the neck bones. Strain the beans over a large pot or bowl to catch the juice; reserve the juice for use in Black Rice. (see p. 41)

Heat the olive oil in a sauté pan until very hot. Quickly sauté the vegetables and herbs until just tender, about 2 to 3 minutes. Add the cumin, cayenne pepper, salt and black pepper and mix well. Place the mixture on a plate and let cool.

Mix the beans with either a mixer with a flat blade paddle, a potato masher or with your hands until the beans are creamed and mashed. Most of the beans will be broken and their mashed starches will come together to bond the cakes. Add the cooled cooked vegetable mixture and mix well. Add the cornbread crumbs and mix well. At this point, you may adjust the salt or spiciness.

Scoop out the mixture with a 1/4 cup measure to make the cakes. Lightly press down to make them about a half-inch thick. Dust lightly in cornmeal.

Pan-fry the cakes in olive oil. Each batch of cakes only needs a couple of Tablespoons of olive oil as it will be absorbed into the cakes. The cakes can be held in a 250 degree oven until all are finished.

If the cakes are made ahead and refrigerated, it is best to bring them back to room temperature before pan-frying.

Serve with Red and Yellow Tomato Salsa (see p. 11) and sour cream or as a starch with selected entrées.

BLACK-EYED PEA CAKES

2 cups dried black-eyed peas, rinsed with cold water

6 cups water

3 chicken bouillon cubes

1 teaspoon salt

1 smoked neck bone

2 Tablespoons olive oil

1/2 cup minced yellow onion

2 tablespoons minced garlic

1/2 cup minced green onions

1/2 cup minced red onion

2 Tablespoons minced cilantro

1/4 cup chopped red pepper

1 Tablespoon stemmed, seeded and minced jalapeño pepper

1 Tablespoon cumin

dash of cayenne pepper

2 teaspoons salt

1 teaspoon freshly ground black pepper

2 cups fresh corn bread crumbs from Corn Bread Recipe (see p. 30)

1 cup olive oil for frying

2 cups stone ground yellow cornmeal for dusting cakes

Black-eyed Pea Cakes were inspired by my good friend and fellow Chef, Richard Perry, who showed me the process of making them. They were a very popular dish when I headed the kitchen at Carolina's and are still on the menu there today.

Makes 24 2-ounce cakes

Using a large, heavy-bottomed saucepan, combine the peas, water, chicken bouillon cubes, salt and smoked neck bones. Bring them to a boil. Reduce to a simmer and cook for 55 minutes or until the peas are very soft and their skins have broken. Add additional water if needed, a cup at a time. Remove the neck bones and strain.

Heat the olive oil in a sauté pan until very hot. Quickly sauté the vegetables until just tender, about 2 to 3 minutes. Add the cumin, cayenne pepper, salt and black pepper. Mix well. Place the mixture on a plate and let cool.

Mix the beans with either a mixer with a flat paddle beater, a potato masher or with your hands until the beans are creamed and mashed. Most of the beans will be broken and their mashed starches wil come together to bond the cakes. Add the cooled cooked vegetable mixture and mix well. Add the corn bread crumbs and mix well. At this point, you may adjust the salt or spiciness.

Scoop out the mixture with a 1/4 cup measure to make cakes. Lightly press them down to make them about a half-inch thick. Dust lightly in cornmeal.

Pan-fry the cakes in olive oil. Each batch of cakes only needs a couple of Tablespoons of olive oil as it will be absorbed into the cakes. The cakes may be held in a 250 degree oven until all are finished.

The cakes may be made ahead and refrigerated. It is best to bring them back to room temperature before pan-frying.

Serve with Sour Cream and Red and Yellow Tomato Salsa or as a starch with selected entrées.

RED AND YELLOW TOMATO SALSA

This recipe makes 6 cups of Red and Yellow Tomato Salsa, which is enough to use with one recipe of Black Bean Cakes or Black-eyed Pea Cakes. If yellow tomatoes are not available, use all red tomatoes. If you prefer to peel your tomatoes, follow the procedure on p.64.

Core the tomatoes. Cut into halves. Lightly squeeze each half without crushing, to remove the seeds, then dice. Place the tomatoes, onions, garlic and basil in a bowl. Add the vinegar, oil, salt and pepper and toss together. Use as needed or place in a storage container and refrigerate. The salsa will keep in the refrigerator for 1 to 2 days.

2½ cups medium diced red tomatoes

2½ cups medium diced yellow tomatoes

1 cup finely diced yellow onions

½ cup thinly sliced green onion

1 Tablespoon minced garlic

½ cup chopped fresh basil

5 Tablespoons red wine vinegar

½ cup plus 2 Tablespoons extra virgin olive oil

1 teaspoon salt

½ teaspoon freshly ground black pepper

PARMESAN FRIED OYSTERS WITH A ROASTED GARLIC DIP

2 dozen oysters, single selects in the shell preferred

12 cups peanut oil (2 48-ounce containers)

1 cup flour

2 eggs

1 teaspoon Dijon mustard

1 teaspoon salt

1 cup fresh dried bread crumbs (see p. 42)

1/2 cup freshly grated Parmesan

1 teaspoon freshly ground black pepper

1 Tablespoon chopped parsley

This is a very flavorful breading for the oysters. The mustard gives them a little tang and the Parmesan makes them even more mouth watering. Be sure to make a lot because they disappear quickly.

Bread the oysters through this 3-step breading process:

•Shuck and drain the liquor from the oysters. Rinse the oysters quickly under cold water. Pat dry with paper towels. Toss the oysters in the flour. Coat the oysters entirely, leaving no wet spots.

•Beat the eggs with the mustard and salt to combine well. Dip the oysters in this mixture. Coat them entirely, leaving no dry spots.

•Combine the bread crumbs, Parmesan, black pepper and parsley. Roll the oysters in the bread crumb mixture. Coat entirely, leaving no wet spots.

Put the peanut oil in a deep fat fryer or a deep frying pan. If you are using something smaller, only use enough oil to fill the fryer about three quarters of the way up the sides. Gradually heat the oil to 340 degrees by starting to heat it on medium and slowly increasing the heat to medium-high. Never put oil in any frying container and turn the heat on to high.

Put a dozen or so oysters into the hot oil at a time. Too many oysters will bring down the temperature of the oil. Try to keep the temperature as close to 340 degrees as possible. Fry the oysters, turning them frequently, until they are golden brown and float to the top. If the oil is too hot, the crust will brown before the oysters cook inside. Remove the oysters from the oil and place on paper towels to absorb any excess oil. Serve at once with homemade Roasted Garlic Dip.

ROASTED GARLIC DIP

The roasted garlic in this dip gives it a great flavor because roasting the garlic makes it surprisingly mild. Peeling the garlic cloves first is an easier method for roasting which also gives you more actual yield. If you are a real garlic lover, you can eat this all by itself as a spread on a good bread.

1/2 cup whole peeled garlic cloves

1 cup mayonnaise

2 Tablespoons roasted garlic

3 Tablespoons finely chopped "bread and butter" pickles (see p. 22)

1 Tablespoon minced shallot

1 Tablespoon finely chopped parsley

1/4 teaspoon salt

1/4 teaspoon freshly ground black pepper

TO ROAST GARLIC:

Preheat an oven to 475 degrees.

Take 1/2 cup of whole, peeled garlic cloves and place them in a small oven-proof skillet or saucepan. Add enough water to bring the water half way up the sides of the garlic cloves. Bring the mixture to a boil, then place the whole pan in the 475 degree oven for about 20 minutes. The water will evaporate and the garlic cloves will take on a light golden color and develop a starchy texture inside.

To be able to measure Tablespoons or teaspoons of roasted garlic, lightly chop the roasted cloves, mash them and then measure. Half a cup of peeled cloves yields approximately 6 Tablespoons of roasted garlic.

TO MAKE THE DIP:

Mix the mayonnaise, 2 Tablespoons of roasted garlic, pickles, shallot, parsley, salt and pepper together. Place in a storage container and refrigerate for at least an hour to let the flavors meld.

DOWN SOUTH EGG ROLLS WITH RED PEPPER SAUCE, SPICY MUSTARD AND PEACH CHUTNEY

Assembling the evening's Specials one day, I knew that I wanted to use chicken, Tasso and collards in some item. As Chef Casey Taylor arrived for work, I tossed it out for his ideas. He quickly suggested an egg roll. After a few adjustments and a lot of egg rolls, it became one of our most popular starters.

Makes 8 egg rolls

Heat the olive oil in a large heavy-bottomed frying pan over medium-high heat. Add the onion, garlic, chicken and Tasso. Sauté, stirring, for 5 minutes or until chicken is fully cooked. Squeeze all juice from the collard greens and add them to the frying pan. Cook for 1 or 2 minutes to heat the collards and meld all of the flavors. Pour into a colander and drain. Spread the mixture out onto a pan and let cool. Then squeeze out as much moisture as you can. You can easily do this by squeezing the mixture in a clean tea towel, in batches if necessary. The drier, the better.

Lay the egg roll wrappers on a clean, dry surface dusted lightly with cornstarch, setting them up in a diamond pattern. Portion 3/4 cup of filling on the centers of each of the 8 wrappers. Place the 2 Tablespoons of cornstarch in a small bowl and slowly add the cold water, stirring until you have a smooth paste which is free of lumps. Lightly brush the edges of each egg roll wrapper with the mixture of cornstarch and water. Fold the bottom quarter of the diamond up toward the top. Fold the two sides inward to form an envelope. Bring the top corner over toward you. Gently press the edges to seal the rolls. Lightly dust the egg rolls with cornstarch to keep them dry.   *(continued on next page)*

2 Tablespoons olive oil

2 cups julienned yellow onion

1 Tablespoon plus 1 teaspoon minced garlic

1 pound boneless, skinless chicken breasts cut into thin strips, removing all fat

1 cup small strips of Tasso

2 packed cups cooked, chopped collard greens, well drained (see p. 48)

8 egg roll wrappers

2 teaspoons cold water

2 Tablespoons cornstarch for sealing

1 cup cornstarch for dusting

12 cups peanut oil or canola oil for frying (2 48-ounce containers)

Put the peanut or canola oil in a deep fryer or a deep frying pan. If you are using something smaller, use only enough oil to fill the fryer about three quarters of the way up the sides. Gradually heat the oil to 340 degrees by starting to heat it on medium heat and slowly increasing the heat to medium-high. Never put oil in any frying container and turn the heat on to high.

Put only 4 egg rolls in the hot oil at the time. Too many egg rolls in the oil will bring down the temperature of the oil. Try to keep the temperature as close to 340 degrees as possible.

Fry, turning frequently, until the egg rolls are golden brown and crispy. Initially you should try to keep the egg rolls submerged. As they brown, they will float to the top. If the oil is too hot, the egg roll skins will brown before the egg rolls become warm throughout. Remove the egg rolls from the oil and place on paper towels to absorb any excess oil.

Serve at once with Red Pepper Sauce, Spicy Mustard and Peach Chutney (see p.17, 18, 19). For 8 egg rolls, you will need $1^1/_2$ cups of each accompaniment.

NOTE: To use chicken thighs, which are less expensive, buy boneless and skinless thighs. Thigh meat will take longer to cook than breast meat. Expect to add another 10 minutes to the sauté procedure.

RED PEPPER SAUCE

Along with the Spicy Mustard and Peach Chutney, this makes the perfect accompaniment for our Down South Egg Roll.

Makes 3¹/₂ cups

Heat the olive oil in a heavy-bottomed saucepan over medium heat. Add the chopped onion and garlic and sauté for 1 minute. Reduce the heat and make a roux by adding the flour and stirring until well combined. Continue to cook over low heat for 2 minutes, stirring constantly. Do not let the onions or flour color. Turn the heat up to medium and add 1¹/₄ cups of the chicken broth, stirring vigorously. Keep stirring vigorously until the broth thickens and is smooth. Gradually add the remaining 1¹/₄ cups of chicken broth, the red pepper strips or the pimiento and the basil, stirring constantly until the broth thickens into a sauce.

Bring the sauce to a low boil, then simmer over medium heat for 10 minutes to cook out the starchy flavor. Skim off any skin that may come to the top. Remove the sauce from the stove and let it cool, stirring occasionally, for 10 minutes. Purée the mixture in a food processor or blender until smooth. Season to taste with salt and cayenne pepper. Use at once or place in a storage container and refrigerate.

Red Pepper Sauce will keep for a week in the refrigerator.

2 Tablespoons plus 1 teaspoon olive oil

¹/₂ cup roughly chopped yellow onion

1 teaspoon roughly chopped garlic

¹/₄ cup flour

2¹/₂ cups chicken broth

1¹/₂ cups red pepper flesh from 3 large roasted red peppers, chopped, or 3 4-ounce cans pimientos, drained and chopped

¹/₄ cup chopped fresh basil

salt and cayenne pepper to taste

SPICY MUSTARD

1 Tablespoon olive oil

$^1/_2$ roughly chopped yellow onion

$^1/_2$ cup roughly chopped
   unpeeled ginger root

1 teaspoon chopped garlic

1 stemmed and chopped
   jalapeño pepper

$^1/_2$ lemon

$^1/_2$ orange

$^1/_2$ cup soy sauce

1 cup Coleman's dry mustard

6 ounces cold water

Makes 1$^1/_2$ cups

Heat the olive oil in a heavy-bottomed saucepan over medium heat to just below the smoking point. Add the onion, ginger, garlic and jalapeño. Sauté for 2 minutes. Cut the lemon and orange into quarters and squeeze the juice over the vegetables. Rough chop the rinds and add them. Add the soy sauce. Cook for 5 minutes over medium heat. Strain and press out the juices.

While this is cooking, place the dry mustard in a small mixing bowl and slowly add the cold water, stirring until you have a smooth paste which is free of lumps. Let this mixture sit for 10 minutes, then stir it into the soy mixture. Use at once or place the mixture in a storage container, let cool at room temperature, cover and refrigerate.

Spicy Mustard will keep for 2–3 weeks in the refrigerator.

PEACH CHUTNEY

While traditional chutneys are thick and jamlike, ours is a lighter, syrupy chutney which allows the peaches to keep their shape, color and texture.

Place all of the ingredients in a heavy-bottomed saucepan over medium heat and stir well to combine. Bring to a boil, stirring, and simmer for 25 to 30 minutes until the chutney begins to thicken slightly and is syrupy. Remove the pan from the heat and let the chutney cool. Use at once or place in a storage container and refrigerate.

Peach Chutney will keep for 2–3 weeks in the refrigerator.

NOTE: If using fresh peaches, select fairly firm ones which are just beginning to ripen and display a peach flavor. Fully ripened fruit will break down in the cooking process.

2 cups peeled fresh or frozen peaches

½ cup minced yellow onion

1 Tablespoon plus 1 teaspoon peeled and finely minced fresh ginger

½ cup finely diced red pepper

½ cup light brown sugar

½ cup white sugar

2 Tablespoons cider vinegar

CRAB DIP WITH GARLIC AND HERB TOASTS

1 Tablespoon olive oil

1 cup finely minced yellow onion

1 Tablespoon finely minced garlic

2 Tablespoons heavy cream

$1/2$ pound cream cheese

1 pound lump crabmeat

1 teaspoon chopped parsley

1 teaspoon chopped basil

1 teaspoon chopped chives

dash of salt, freshly ground black pepper and cayenne pepper

Makes 2 cups

Heat the olive oil in a heavy-bottomed sauce pan over medium heat. Add the onions and garlic and sauté for 2 minutes, stirring to prevent browning. Add the heavy cream and stir to combine. Add the cream cheese and whisk until all of the cheese is melted and you have a smooth mixture.

Remove the pan from the heat and place the mixture in a bowl. Let it cool for 10 minutes at room temperature. Fold in the crabmeat, herbs and seasonings. Serve immediately or refrigerate and serve chilled. Accompany with Herb Toasts.

NOTE: All crabmeat should be gently picked over to remove any possible remaining shell. Place the crabmeat in a strainer and press down lightly to extract any extra water. When using lump crab, you want to keep it as intact as possible.

HERB TOASTS

$3/4$ cup olive oil

2 teaspoons mashed garlic

1 Tablespoon very finely minced chives

1 Tablespoon very finely minced basil

1 Tablespoon very finely minced parsley

$1/2$ teaspoon salt

$1/2$ teaspoon freshly ground black pepper

1 long loaf of fresh, crusty French bread

I would recommend that you serve this fresh, crisp toast with the Crab Dip. The herbed olive oil brushed on the bread is mild and does not distract from the crab flavor of the dip.

Preheat oven to 350 degrees.

Combine all of the ingredients except the French bread and let them sit for 15 minutes. Slice the bread into thin slices. Lay the slices on a baking sheet and brush the tops with the herbed olive oil. Bake the slices at 350 degrees for 8 to 10 minutes or until they are crisply toasted and light golden in color.

SWEET PEPPER RELISH

Just a simple sweet relish, this accompanies pork and chicken quite well.

Makes 1 cup

Place the red peppers, green peppers, jalapeños, lime juice and sugar in a heavy-bottomed saucepan over medium heat. Stir until the sugar is dissolved and the peppers release their juices. Cook, stirring occasionally, until the relish reduces in volume by about one third. The syrup will foam and form many bubbles as it gets near the desired consistency.

Remove the relish from the heat and pour it into a glass, crockery or stainless steel storage container. Let cool at room temperature then add the cilantro. As it cools, the relish will thicken. Cover and refrigerate it. The relish will keep in the refrigerator for 3 weeks.

1 cup finely diced red peppers

1 cup finely diced green peppers

1 Tablespoon stemmed, seeded and minced jalapeño pepper

3 Tablespoons fresh lime juice

³/₄ cup sugar

1 Tablespoon minced cilantro

BREAD AND BUTTER PICKLES

12 cucumbers, washed and cut in ¹/₂-inch thick slices

2 cups of julienned yellow onions

¹/₄ cup salt

4 cups sugar

4 cups cider vinegar

1 Tablespoon yellow mustard seed

¹/₂ teaspoon turmeric

2 teaspoons celery seed

My mother's recipe for these crunchy cucumber disks makes a great accompaniment to sandwiches and salads. They also are a fine mid-afternoon snack all by themselves.

Makes 1 gallon

Toss the cucumbers and onions in a stainless steel, glass or crockery bowl. Add the ¹/₂ cup of salt and toss. Cover them completely with ice cubes and let sit for 3 hours.

Combine the sugar, cider vinegar, mustard seed, turmeric and celery seed in a heavy-bottomed stockpot. Bring to a boil, stirring. Pour the cucumber and onion mixture into a colander and rinse with cold water. Drain well. Place the drained cucumbers and onions into the stockpot with the boiling sugar and vinegar mixture and bring to a boil again. Reduce the heat to medium and simmer for 5 minutes, stirring occasionally.

Remove the stockpot from the stove and pour the pickles into a glass or crockery storage container. Let the pickles cool at room temperature, cover and refrigerate.

The pickles will keep in the refrigerator for 3–4 weeks.

TOASTED SPICED PECANS

These pecans make a wonderful cocktail snack and a good enhancement when crumbled over salads. Try this with fresh pecans in the fall, when they are at the peak of their season, to really see them at their best.

Preheat oven to 350 degrees.

Melt the butter in a saucepan over medium heat. Stir in the pecans, cayenne pepper and salt. Cook the pecans in the butter mixture, stirring continually for 1 minute and being careful not to let the pecans burn.

Spread the pecans out on a baking sheet. Bake at 350 degrees for 4 minutes. They should be shiny with a lightly toasted aroma, color and flavor. Remove the pecans from the oven and place on paper towels to absorb excess oil. Cool to room temperature and store in an air-tight container.

1 Tablespoon unsalted butter

1 cup pecan halves (about $1/2$ pound)

$1/8$ teaspoon cayenne pepper

$1/4$ teaspoon salt

CHEESE ENCRUSTED WADMALAW SWEET ONIONS WITH A CARAMELIZED ONION AND THYME BROTH

1 Tablespoon olive oil

4 cups of julienned sweet or yellow onions

2 teaspoons minced garlic

2 teaspoons fresh thyme leaves or 1 teaspoon dried thyme

1/2 teaspoon freshly ground black pepper

2 Tablespoons sherry wine vinegar or sherry wine

5 cups chicken broth

1 Tablespoon Worcestershire sauce

4 servings

Inspired by the onions that my father roasted in the oven with butter and black pepper, I recreated this dish to celebrate the sweet onions which come in the late spring. For the whole onions, you won't get the sweetness of the Wadmalaw with the winter white or yellow onions. You may, however, substitute other sweet onions such as Vidalia or Maui. For the broth, the regular onions work because they are combined with all of the other ingredients.

FOR THE ONION BROTH:

Heat the olive oil in a heavy-bottomed stock pot over high heat until the oil is smoking. Carefully drop the julienned onions into the oil. Leave the onions there for a minute or two without stirring. The natural sugars in the onions will begin to caramelize and they will turn a golden color. Stir the onions. Add a little more oil, 1 teaspoon at a time, if the oil has disappeared. Continue to cook, stirring frequently, until the onions are golden brown.

Reduce the heat to medium. Add the garlic, thyme and black pepper to the onions. Cook, stirring, for about 2 minutes. Add the sherry wine vinegar or sherry to deglaze the bottom of the pan and scrape up any onion caramelization. Do not worry if some onions are blackened in a few places. It takes a good caramelized color to make the broth hearty and robust.

Add the chicken broth and Worcestershire sauce. Bring the broth to a boil, reduce to a simmer and let simmer for 10 to 15 minutes. Remove any foam that may appear. Remove the stock pot to the back of the stove to keep warm.

FOR THE CHEESE ENCRUSTED ROASTED ONIONS:

When you are selecting your onions, try to uniformly choose tennis ball size so that they will cook evenly. Peel the onions carefully, not cutting deeply on the bottom so that there is enough root structure left to hold the onion together. Try not to cut into the outer layer. This will also help to keep the onion whole.

Preheat oven to 375 degrees.

Take the 4 peeled onions and cut out a cone shaped core in the top half of each that goes about $1/4$-inch into the onion and is about the diameter of a half dollar.

Combine the cheddar, blue cheese, Parmesan, thyme, parsley, chives and black pepper for the filling. Fill the cut-out holes in the onions with the cheese mixture, leaving some to make a final crust. Place the onions in a 9" by 9" baking pan and add the chicken broth, thyme and garlic. This should come up to about $1/4$-inch high on the sides of the onions.

Spray a piece of aluminum foil with non-stick spray. Lightly cover the pan, not letting the foil touch the tops of the onions if possible. Place the pan on the top shelf of the 375 degree oven and bake for 1 hour.

Remove the onions from the roasting broth and discard the broth. Place the onions back in the pan and top with the remaining cheese mixture. Broil until the cheese becomes golden brown.

Check the seasoning of the onion broth which has been kept warm on the back of the stove. Ladle $3/4$ cup of the onion broth into each of 4 shallow soup plates. Place the hot cheese-filled onions in the plates and serve.

4 whole, peeled sweet onions

$1/2$ cup grated good quality New York or Vermont sharp cheddar cheese

$1/4$ cup good Danish Blue or Roquefort cheese

$1/2$ cup freshly grated Parmesan

1 teaspoon fresh thyme

1 teaspoon chopped parsley

1 teaspoon chopped chives

$1/4$ teaspoon freshly ground black pepper

1 cup chicken broth

2 sprigs of fresh thyme or a sprinkle of dried thyme

1 teaspoon minced garlic

NOTE: While there are many quality cheddars in the market-place, for uniformity of flavor and cooking consistency, I have had the most success with Kraft Cracker Barrel New York or Vermont sharp Cheddar, which is available nationwide.

PAN-FRIED CHICKEN LIVERS WITH CARAMELIZED ONIONS, COUNTRY HAM AND RED-EYE GRAVY

1 Tablespoon olive oil

2 cups of raw yellow onion, cut into ¹/₄-inch slices (1 large onion)

2 cups chicken livers (about 1 pound) Select nice looking, firm livers which have a deep dark color.

¹/₂ cup flour

1 teaspoon salt

1 teaspoon black pepper

2 Tablespoons olive oil

6 ounces of very thinly sliced country ham

To make these livers really "Uptown," serve them with the Madeira Sauce, which takes a good deal of preparation, but which is well worth it. Otherwise, more "Down South," but also fine, the Red-Eye Gravy is quicker.

4 servings

ONIONS:
Heat 1 teaspoon of olive oil in a heavy-bottomed frying pan over high heat until the oil is smoking. Lay the onion slices in the hot oil. You want to keep the slices intact and not loosen them into rings until after the initial searing. Leave them there for 1 or 2 minutes without turning to start the caramelization process. Cook, tossing occasionally, until the onions caramelize and turn golden brown. At this point the slices may break out into rings. Watch the heat and reduce it slightly if it appears that the onions are beginning to burn. A teaspoon of the oil may be added if the pan becomes dry and the bottom begins to scorch. The caramelization process should take 6 to 10 minutes. When the onions have browned, remove them from the heat until ready to serve.

LIVERS AND HAM:
Preheat oven to 350 degrees.

Trim any fat or sinew from the chicken livers. Rinse under cold water, then leave them in a bowl of cold water for 5 minutes to remove any residual blood. Remove the livers from the water and place them on absorbent paper towels to drain. Any excess water will splatter when the chicken livers are placed in the hot oil.

Combine the flour, salt and black pepper, mixing well. Dust the chicken livers with the seasoned flour, making certain to cover them completely so that there are no wet spots showing. Shake off any excess flour so that it does not burn in the pan.

Heat the olive oil in a heavy-bottomed frying pan over medium-high heat. Gently place the livers in the hot oil. They will spit and splatter in the oil. Cover with a lid or splatter guard. Sauté them on one side for 1 to 2 minutes until golden. Uncover the pan, flip the livers over and shake the pan. If all of the oil has been absorbed, add a little more a teaspoon at a time.

Put the livers in the 350 oven for 3 to 4 minutes or until they are firm and their centers are cooked through. While the livers are cooking, sauté the ham in a heavy-bottomed frying pan over medium heat until the ham's edges curl up. Add the caramelized onions to the frying pan to reheat while the livers are cooking.

When ready to serve, remove the livers from the oven. Place the livers on a plate and place the ham around them. Mound the onions in the center. Spoon Madeira Sauce (see p. 113) or Red-Eye Gravy (see p. 74) around the ham, livers and onions. Serve immediately.

NOTE: The caramelized onions could be cooked ahead. However, the livers and ham are best when cooked right before serving.

BAR-B-QUED SHRIMP

1 teaspoon olive oil

1 teaspoon Magnolias'
 Blackening Spice (see p. 64)

1 teaspoon minced garlic

1 pound medium or large peeled
 and deveined shrimp

4 servings

Fire your grill.

Combine the olive oil, Blackening Spice and garlic. Toss the shrimp in this mixture. Skewer the shrimp between 2 skewers.

Grill the shrimp over high heat for 4 to 6 minutes, or until they have turned pink and are firm and plump. Brush with Magnolias' Bar-B-Que Sauce (see p.108).

NOTE: When grilling, the cook is always wise to fix a little more than the needed amount to allow for testing.

PIMIENTO CHEESE

One of my best friends' mother, and my best critic, Alice Marks, makes the quintessential Pimiento Cheese. I have never seen her recipe, so this is about as close as I can get to duplicating her "Southern Caviar." I prefer to use the fresh roasted red pepper. It gives enough extra depth and flavor to be worth the 50 minute roasting and peeling process. If you prefer a spicy version, add 1 Tablespoon sautéed minced jalapeño pepper and a few dashes of hot sauce.

Makes 2¹/₂ cups

Combine all of the ingredients in a glass, crockery or stainless steel mixing bowl and mix well. Season to taste with cayenne pepper. Refrigerate until ready to serve.

ROASTED PEPPERS

Preheat oven to 500 degrees.

Wash, drain and dry the peppers. Rub the peppers with olive oil by hand, just to coat them lightly. Place the peppers on a baking pan and roast on the top shelf of the 500 degree oven for about 25 minutes, turning once or twice. The skin should be well blistered and will be blackened in some places.

Remove the peppers from the oven. Place them in a small bowl and cover it tightly with plastic wrap. Let the peppers cool for 10 to 15 minutes. The skin will become loose and easy to remove. Peel the skin off of the peppers. Remove the stems, cores and seeds. Do not rinse. At this point you may use the peppers in any manner that you would use pimientos.

NOTE: Thin peppers will have a shorter roasting time. It's preferable to use fresh peppers that look very healthy and have good thick flesh.

5 large roasted red peppers or 2¹/₂ cups diced medium red pimientos

1 cup stuffed green olives, finely chopped

1¹/₄ pounds good quality New York or Vermont sharp white cheddar cheese, grated (see p. 25)

¹/₄ cup freshly grated Parmesan cheese

¹/₄ cup mayonnaise

1 Tablespoon chopped fresh parsley

¹/₂ teaspoon freshly ground black pepper

dash of cayenne pepper, or to taste

YELLOW CORN BISCUITS

1 cup fresh raw yellow corn kernels

6 Tablespoons heavy cream

8 Tablespoons cold, diced unsalted butter

1 cup coarsely ground yellow corn meal

2$\frac{1}{2}$ cups all-purpose flour

1 Tablespoon plus 1 teaspoon non-alum baking powder (see p. 31)

3 Tablespoons sugar

1 teaspoon salt

$\frac{1}{2}$ teaspoon freshly ground black pepper

1 egg

$\frac{1}{2}$ cup plus 2 Tablespoons buttermilk

extra flour for rolling out the biscuits

2 Tablespoons unsalted butter, melted

These biscuits are an inspiration from Don Drake. We put Bar-B-Que in bite-size versions and served them as hors d'oeuvre at our "Carolina Christmas" dinner at the James Beard House.

14-2$\frac{1}{2}$-inch biscuits

Cut the raw corn kernels off of the corn cobs. Scrape the cobs over a bowl to release all of the corn's "milk." Lightly chop the kernels. In a heavy-bottomed sauce pan, combine the corn, the corn "milk" and the heavy cream. Cook over medium heat for 4 or 5 minutes or until the cream is reduced to one third of its original volume. It will be thick and creamy. Set aside and let cool at room temperature. Process the corn mixture lightly or mash it to break up the kernels.

Preheat oven to 400 degrees. Dice the butter, put it on a plate and put it back into the refrigerator to remain cold while you are assembling the other ingredients. Combine the cornmeal, flour, baking powder, sugar, salt, and pepper. Add the diced butter and cut it into the flour with either a pastry cutter or 2 forks until the butter is reduced to the size of the cornmeal. This should be done quickly so that the butter doesn't get too warm or melt.

Beat the egg and the buttermilk together. Mix the creamed corn with the egg and buttermilk. Add this mixture into the flour mixture a little at a time until the dough comes together. It may be a bit wet, but it can be handled easily with a light dusting of flour. Place the dough on a floured board and round it out with your hands. Pat the round out to a thickness of $\frac{1}{2}$ inch. Cut the biscuits with a 2$\frac{1}{2}$ inch cutter.

Place the biscuits on a baking sheet and bake at the top of the 400 degree oven for 15 to 20 minutes or until they are golden brown and cooked through. Remove the baking sheet from the oven and brush the tops of the biscuits with the 2 Tablespoons of melted butter. Serve at once.

CORN BREAD

This basic corn bread recipe is best when cooked in a seasoned cast iron skillet. The crust that the cast iron produces is one which you can only obtain with this historic cook ware.

Preheat oven to 425 degrees.

If you are using a cast iron skillet, as soon as the oven reaches 425 degrees, place the skillet in the oven and let the skillet preheat. This is what makes the good, brown bottom crust.

Mix the cornmeal, flour, baking powder, salt and sugar. Lightly beat the eggs and whisk into the buttermilk. Fold the buttermilk mixture into the dry mixture. Stir in the melted butter.

If you are using a cast iron skillet, remove it from the oven and rub it with additional oil to coat it lightly. Pour the corn bread batter into the pan or the preheated skillet.

Bake the corn bread on the top shelf of the 425 degree oven for about 25 minutes or until the top is brown, the center is firm and a knife inserted into the center comes out clean.

Remove the corn bread from the oven and let it sit in the pan or skillet for 8 to 10 minutes to cool slightly before cutting to serve.

NOTE: Non-alum baking powder is one which contains no sodium aluminum sulfate and consequently lacks the metallic taste that it imparts. The most easily found grocery store brand is Rumford.

1 seasoned, well oiled 12" cast iron skillet

or

1 well oiled 9" x 13" baking pan

peanut oil for oiling pan or skillet

2 cups stone-ground yellow cornmeal

1¼ cups plus 2 Tablespoons all-purpose flour

1 Tablespoon plus 1 teaspoon non-alum baking powder

½ teaspoon salt

5 Tablespoons sugar

4 eggs

2 cups buttermilk

5 Tablespoons unsalted butter, melted

CORN BREAD STYX

1 Tablespoon finely chopped red pepper

1 Tablespoon finely chopped green onion

1 Tablespoon finely chopped red onion

1 teaspoon stemmed, seeded and finely minced jalapeño pepper

1 Tablespoon finely chopped cilantro

$1/2$ cup cooked fresh yellow corn kernels (see p. 67)

$1/4$ teaspoon minced garlic

$1/2$ teaspoon cumin

$1/2$ teaspoon freshly ground black pepper

$1/2$ cup grated good quality New York or Vermont sharp white cheddar cheese

1 cup stone-ground yellow cornmeal

$1/2$ cup plus 2 Tablespoons all-purpose flour

2 teaspoons non-alum baking powder (see p. 31)

$1/4$ teaspoon salt

$2 1/2$ Tablespoons sugar

2 eggs

1 cup buttermilk

$2 1/2$ Tablespoons unsalted butter, melted

The vegetable and cheese additions to the corn bread batter give an interesting texture to the corn bread. At the restaurant, we also serve these corn bread styx with a starter of Pork Bar-B-Que and Mustard Slaw.

14 corn bread styx

2 well-seasoned cast iron corn stick molds

Preheat oven to 500 degrees. Put the corn stick pans in the oven and heat for 10 minutes. Remove, spray with non-stick baking spray and reduce the oven heat to 400 degrees.

Combine the red pepper, green onion, red onion, jalapeño pepper, cilantro, corn kernels, garlic, cumin, black pepper and white cheddar cheese. Mix well. Set aside while making the corn bread batter.

Mix the cornmeal, flour, baking powder, salt and sugar. Lightly beat the eggs and whisk them into the buttermilk. Fold buttermilk mixture into the dry mixture. Stir in the melted butter. Fold in the vegetable and spice mixture.

Reduce the heat to 400 degrees. Each stick in the mold takes approximately $1/4$ cup of batter. The pans should be hot enough so that the batter sizzles when it hits the pan. Bake the corn styx at 400 degrees on the top shelf of the oven for 20 to 25 minutes, or until golden brown on the top and cooked through. Remove the pans from the oven and allow the corn styx to cool for 5 minutes. Remove the styx from the pans by tapping the pans on their sides. The styx will fall out of the pans. Serve at once.

COUNTRY CORN BREAD

This flavorful cornbread takes a little more work, but if you serve it with eggs, or as part of a brunch or a Southern dinner, you'll be sold.

1 seasoned, well oiled 12" cast iron skillet or 1 well oiled 9" x 13" baking pan

Preheat oven to 425 degrees.

If you are using a cast iron skillet, as soon as the oven reaches 425 degrees, place the cast iron skillet in the oven and let the skillet preheat. This is what makes for a good, brown bottom crust.

In a large skillet or frying pan, cook the chopped bacon until it is crisp and lightly browned. Add the sausage and vegetables and sauté for 1 to 2 minutes. Add the freshly ground pepper. Remove the pan from the stove and let the mixture cool slightly.

Mix the cornmeal, flour, baking powder, salt and sugar. Lightly beat the eggs and whisk into the buttermilk. Fold the buttermilk mixture into the dry mixture. Stir in the melted butter. Stir in the bacon, sausage and vegetable mixture.

If you are using a cast iron skillet, remove it from the oven and rub with additional oil to lightly coat the inside. Pour the corn bread batter into the pan or preheated skillet. Bake the corn bread on the top shelf of the oven for about 25 minutes or until the top is brown, the center is firm and a knife inserted into the center comes out clean. Let the corn bread sit in the pan or skillet for 8 to 10 minutes to cool slightly before cutting to serve.

Peanut oil for oiling the pan or skillet

1/4 pound chopped smoked bacon (about 8 strips)

1 cup spicy breakfast sausage, cooked, drained, cooled and crumbled

1 cup cooked fresh yellow corn kernels (about 2 ears) (see p. 67)

1/2 cup finely diced red peppers

1/2 cup finely sliced green onions

1/2 cup finely diced red onion

1 teaspoon garlic

1 Tablespoon coarsely ground peppercorns

2 cups stone-ground yellow cornmeal

1 1/4 cups all-purpose flour

1 Tablespoon and 1 teaspoon non-alum baking powder (see p. 31)

1/2 teaspoon salt

5 Tablespoons sugar

4 eggs

2 cups buttermilk

1 Tablespoon unsalted butter, melted

VEGETABLES, RICE
GREENS AND BEANS

VEGETABLES, RICE, GREENS AND BEANS

If you add the Grits from the next chapter, you have the backbone of true Southern cooking. My love for this food began in my younger years when I was growing up in Charleston, West Virginia. While I started with baking, I soon began to notice all kinds of food, especially that of my grandparents' garden. My grandparents on my father's side lived a very simple life and grew most of what they ate right there. I looked forward to our weekend visits, especially to going out to the garden to check the progress of their crops. They grew everything from corn to peanuts, cabbage to strawberries, and five kinds of tomatoes.

Vegetables stayed a part of every step of my way toward the menu at Magnolias. For my first real job in the hospitality industry, I began as a prep cook/stock person at the restaurant of a friend of my father's. I did potato skins by the thousands, cleaned spinach by the ton and cut onions until my tear ducts were dried. As you prepare my food, you will see that I use the produce of our region. There are a couple of occasions when I suggest a substitution of canned tomatoes, but that's only when a good quality canned tomato is preferable to a pale, tasteless winter tomato. You'll also notice throughout the book that we use a lot of fresh corn at Magnolias. Once you taste our local varieties, you'll know why.

Greens are the same—collards and mustards, that is. We use all of the local greens available, but we always use fresh greens, even when we have to get them from other areas. Please note that I cook our greens with chicken broth. You'll be surprised how much that complements the flavor. Instead of using fatback in the greens, I prefer to use a much less fatty smoked neck bone or ham hock. While this can certainly be left out completely, it does adds a subtle smoky flavor which enhances many dishes.

Rice is almost as important to Southern cuisine as is corn. A major crop years ago, rice remains a staple. We have some fun with it at Magnolias. While I thought Black Rice perhaps to be our invention, I have found the concept of it in other cookbooks. At any rate, what we are seeing is evidence of the popularity of using the juice from cooking black beans.

Butter beans are another favorite vegetable indigenous to the South. They do not taste the same as baby limas. If they aren't grown in your part of the country, take a look in the frozen food section of your grocery store. As mentioned in our recipe for butter beans as a side dish, you'll have to make a slight adjustment for cooking frozen ones. In the South, we value our heritage and stick to our array of "Sides," that endless number of little dishes which have long been a part of Southern cooking. At Magnolias, they have always been a serious part of our menu.

BUTTERMILK MASHED POTATOES

Using a potato ricer for making mashed potatoes is the preferable method because it produces an end result that is very smooth. It is one of those old fashioned pieces of kitchen equipment that still does the best job.

8 servings

Place the potatoes, water and salt in a large, heavy saucepan over medium heat. Bring them to a boil and cook for about 30 minutes, or until very tender. Pour the potatoes into a colander and drain. Toss them briefly with a wooden spoon to release the steam.

Run the potatoes through a potato ricer or place them in the bowl of an electric mixer and whip with the flat paddle attachment, stopping periodically to scrape down the sides. The potatoes should be free of all lumps before any liquid is added. Melt the butter in the milk and add this to the potatoes. Add the buttermilk. Season to taste. Serve immediately.

12 baking potatoes, peeled, sliced lengthwise and cut in 1/2-inch pieces

8 cups water

1 Tablespoon salt

6 Tablespoons unsalted butter

6 ounces whole milk, scalded

6 ounces buttermilk, room temperature

salt and freshly ground black pepper

PARSLIED POTATOES

20 small red new potatoes (golf ball size)

1 teaspoon salt

1 teaspoon olive oil

salt

freshly ground black pepper

2 Tablespoons finely chopped parsley

6 servings.

With a small knife, cut off the tops and bottoms of the potatoes and pare down the sides, giving them an oval shape.

Place the potatoes, enough water to cover them and the 1 teaspoon of salt in a saucepan over medium heat. Bring them to a boil. Reduce to a simmer and simmer for 15 minutes or until tender. It is important not to boil the potatoes roughly because it will cook the outside before the inside.

Place ice cubes in a bowl of cold water and set aside. Drain the potatoes. Rinse them with cold water and immerse in the ice water to stop the cooking. Drain and pat dry. Heat the olive oil in a heavy bottomed skillet over medium high heat. Roll the potatoes in the hot oil to lightly brown the outside and warm them through.

Add salt and pepper to taste and parsley to please the eye.

DIRTY RICE

This is a hearty rice with lots of depth. The chicken livers give it both flavor and nutritional value. True to its name, it looks dirty, but tastes just fine.

4-6 servings

Preheat oven to 350 degrees

Toss the livers, 1 teaspoon of the olive oil, and a dash of salt and pepper in a glass, crockery or stainless bowl. Place the livers on a baking sheet with sides and place it on the top rack of the 350 degree oven. Bake them for 20 minutes. Cool the livers, finely chop them and set aside.

Heat the remaining 3 Tablespoons of olive oil in a heavy-bottomed saucepan over medium heat.. Add the onions and garlic and sauté, stirring, for 2 to 3 minutes, or until the onions are translucent. Add the sausage, Tasso and chicken livers and sauté for 3 minutes. Add the rice and stir until it is coated by the olive oil.

Pour in the chicken broth and bring the mixture to a boil, constantly stirring. Cover the saucepan and place it in the 350 degree oven. Bake the rice for 20 to 30 minutes or until all of the liquid is absorbed and the rice is tender. Uncover the saucepan, add the green onions and fluff the rice and onions with a fork. Season with salt, black pepper and Tabasco to taste.

Serve immediately.

1/2 cup chopped, cooked chicken livers (about 1/4 pound raw livers)

3 Tablespoons plus one teaspoon olive oil

salt and freshly ground black pepper to taste

1/2 cup finely chopped yellow onions

1 Tablespoon minced garlic

1/2 cup spicy Italian sausage (6 ounces raw) (see p. 72)

1/4 cup chopped Tasso

2 cups converted rice

2 3/4 cups chicken broth

1/2 cup chopped green onions

2 to 3 dashes Tabasco

RED RICE

6 ounces tomato juice

14 ounces chicken broth

2 Tablespoons tomato paste

$\frac{1}{2}$ teaspoon salt

$\frac{1}{4}$ teaspoon freshly ground black
    pepper

dash of cayenne pepper

3 ounces olive oil

$\frac{1}{2}$ cup chopped yellow onions

1 Tablespoon minced garlic

$\frac{1}{2}$ cup chopped celery

$\frac{1}{4}$ cup chopped cooked spicy
    Italian sausage (3-ounces raw)
    (see p. 72)

$\frac{1}{4}$ cup finely chopped Tasso

2 cups converted rice

Enhanced with sausage, Tasso and tomato juice, this spicy rice is a good side dish with chicken, pork and seafood.

4-6 servings

Preheat oven to 350 degrees.

Combine the tomato juice, chicken broth, tomato paste, salt, black pepper and cayenne pepper, and reserve. In a heavy-bottomed stockpot, heat the olive oil over medium heat. Add the onions, garlic, celery, sausage and Tasso. Sauté, stirring, for 2 to 3 minutes or until the onions are translucent. Add the rice and stir until the rice is coated with oil. Pour in the tomato juice mixture. Bring to a boil, constantly stirring.

Cover the stockpot and place it in the 350 degree oven. Bake the rice for about 20 minutes, or until all of the liquid is absorbed and the rice is tender. Uncover the stock pot, fluff the rice with a fork and season with more salt, black pepper or cayenne pepper if desired.

Serve immediately.

BLACK RICE

This resourceful recipe makes use of the liquid that results from cooking the black beans in the black bean cake recipe. Use the resulting sediment as a part of the liquid also; it imparts color and flavor. If you are short on the black bean liquid, add chicken broth to reach the needed quantity.

6 servings

Preheat oven to 350 degrees.

Combine the black bean juice with the chicken bouillon cubes and the cumin in a heavy-bottomed saucepan over medium heat. Bring this to a boil. Heat the olive oil in a large, heavy-bottomed stockpot over medium heat. Add the onion and garlic and sauté for 1 minute. Add the rice and toss to coat with oil. Pour the boiling black bean juice over the rice, stir and bring the mixture back to a boil.

Cover the stockpot and put it in the pre-heated oven. Bake the rice for 20 to 30 minutes, or until all of the liquid is absorbed and the rice is tender. Uncover the stockpot, fluff the rice with a fork and season with salt if desired.

Serve immediately.

3 cups black bean juice (see p. 8)

2 chicken bouillon cubes

2 teaspoons cumin

2 Tablespoons olive oil

1 cup minced yellow onion

1 teaspoon minced garlic

$2^1/_4$ cups converted rice

salt to taste

FRIED ASPARAGUS WITH WHITE CHEDDAR CHEESE SAUCE

2 bunches medium-sized fresh asparagus (30 to 32 spears), white ends trimmed off to make 4 to 5 inch long spears

12 cups peanut oil (2 48-ounce bottles)

1 cup flour

2 eggs

1 Tablespoon of water

2 Tablespoons Dijon or whole grain mustard

1 teaspoon salt

1 cup fresh dried bread crumbs

1/4 cup freshly grated Parmesan

1 Tablespoon chopped parsley

1 Tablespoon chopped basil

1/2 teaspoon black pepper

NOTE: To make fresh dried bread crumbs, use a good quality white bread like Pepperidge Farms. Trim the crust off. Place the bread on a baking sheet and put it on the upper rack of a 225 degree oven for 10 to 12 minutes or until the bread is dry throughout. To crumble, run through a food processor or grate by hand.

Working with the ever-present asparagus, I was trying to think of an interesting twist. A spontaneous suggestion from a passing kitchen worker was that I should fry them. The crispy breading complements the pencil-like vegetable very well.

6 Servings: about 5 to 6 spears per person

Bread the asparagus by this 3-step breading process:

•Rinse the asparagus in cold water. Shake off any excess liquid. While the asparagus are still damp, toss them in the flour. Coat the asparagus entirely, leaving no wet spots.

•Beat the eggs with the water, mustard and salt to combine well. Dip the asparagus in this mixture. Coat them entirely, leaving no dry spots.

•Combine the bread crumbs, Parmesan, parsley, basil and black pepper. Roll the asparagus in the bread crumb mixture. Coat entirely, leaving no wet spots.

Put the peanut oil in a deep fat fryer or a deep frying pan. If you are using something smaller, use only enough oil to fill the fryer about three quarters of the way up the sides. Gradually heat the oil to between 310 and 325 degree by starting to heat it on medium heat and slowly increasing the heat to medium-high. Never put oil in any frying container and turn the heat on to high.

Put 6 or 8 asparagus in the hot oil at a time. Too many asparagus will bring down the temperature of the oil. Try to stay evenly within this range. Fry the asparagus until they are golden brown. If the oil is too hot, the crust will brown before the asparagus cooks throughout.

Remove the asparagus from the oil and place on paper towels for a moment to absorb any excess oil. Serve at once with White Cheddar Cheese Sauce.

WHITE CHEDDAR CHEESE SAUCE

This sauce can easily scorch because it is largely composed of dairy products. It should be carefully watched while cooking. If you are not using the sauce right away, keep it covered with a lid or with plastic wrap to prevent a skin from forming.

Makes 3 cups, which is enough for 6 servings of Fried Asparagus

In a heavy-bottomed saucepan, melt the butter over low heat. Add the garlic and sauté for 1 minute, stirring constantly to prevent browning. Make a roux by adding the flour and stirring until well combined. Continue to cook over low heat for 5 minutes, stirring very frequently to prevent browning. Turn the heat up to medium and add 1 cup of the milk, stirring vigorously. Keep stirring constantly until the sauce begins to thicken and is smooth. Gradually add the remaining $1^1/4$ cups of milk, stirring constantly until the sauce rethickens. Add the bay leaf. Let the sauce simmer over very low heat for about 5 minutes, stirring frequently, until the starchy taste is cooked out. Remove the bay leaf. Add the cheese and stir until well blended.

Taste for seasoning. Stir in the $^1/4$ teaspoon of salt and dash of cayenne pepper, or add more to taste.

2 Tablespoons unsalted butter

1 teaspoon minced garlic

$^1/4$ cup flour

$2^1/4$ cups milk

1 bay leaf

2 lightly packed cups of grated good quality New York or Vermont sharp white cheddar cheese (6 oz.) (see p. 25)

$^1/4$ teaspoon salt

dash of cayenne pepper

43

MARINATED, GRILLED VEGETABLES

The most important thing to remember about grilling is that most grills produce somewhat different results. The cooking times for these vegetables are based upon grilling them on a gas grill on high heat with the lid down. Keeping the lid closed on a grill will help to bake the vegetables through. Use these times as guidelines for the first time that you grill vegetables. Then take note of what to expect from your own grill.

Select medium sized vegetables. You should cut them about an inch thick because they will shrink a bit when they are grilled. I prefer moist, tender, lightly charred grilled vegetables with a well-seasoned, garlicky flavor.

The marinade is just enough to give the vegetables a light oily sheen. This prevents oil from dripping onto the heat source, flaming up and producing a black soot which is neither healthy or appetizing. A light rub with the marinade will end in better tasting results.

MARINADE:
1 teaspoon olive oil
1 teaspoon minced garlic
$1/8$ teaspoon freshly ground black pepper
dash of salt
This marinade will be a sufficient amount for any of the following vegetables:

BELL PEPPERS: 3 large bell peppers, stem, rib and seeds removed and cut into quarters. Toss with the marinade. Grill for about 5 minutes, turning once.

ASPARAGUS: 1 bunch, white ends removed. Toss with the marinade. Grill for 8 to 10 minutes, turning so that all sides are grilled.

ZUCCHINI: 2 medium zucchini, stems removed and split in half lengthwise into slices that are about 1 inch thick. Toss with the marinade. Grill for about 20 minutes, turning once.

YELLOW SQUASH: 2 medium yellow squash, stems removed and split in half lengthwise into slices that are about 1 inch thick. Toss with the marinade. Grill for about 20 minutes, turning once.

GREEN ONIONS: 1 bunch of 6 to 8, roots and tips of green ends removed. Toss with the marinade. Grill for about 2 minutes, turning so that all sides are grilled.

YELLOW ONIONS: 2 medium onions, peeled and cut into slices that are about $1/2$-inch thick. Rub with the marinade instead of tossing so that you can try to keep the slices intact. Grill for 20 to 25 minutes, turning once.

SWEET POTATOES: Preheat an oven to 350 degrees. Rub the skin of 2 sweet potatoes with olive oil. Bake at 350 degrees for 30 minutes for a large potato, (about the size of a baking potato). It should still be firm enough to handle. Undercooking the sweet potato will allow it to be firm enough to hold together when cut in half and will also allow you to grill it easily. Toss the sweet potato halves with the marinade. Grill for about 5 minutes, turning over.

TOMATOES: 2 large tomatoes, cut across into slices that are about $1/4$ inch thick. Rub with the marinade. Grill for 3 to 4 minutes, gently turning once.

CORN ON THE COB: Peel the husks back, but do not pull or cut them off. Remove the corn silk, rub the ear with the marinade and a little extra salt. Each ear will take a full recipe of marinade so you should go ahead and make enough for the number of ears that you are going to grill. Sprinkle the ear with a little cold water. Pull the husks back up over the ear. Wrap the corn in foil and twist up the ends to seal it. Roast on a hot grill for 15 to 20 minutes.

EGGPLANT: 2 eggplant, cut into slices that are about 1 inch thick.
Whisk the following ingredients together to make a marinade:
2 Tablespoons soy sauce
2 Tablespoons oil
1 teaspoon minced garlic
pinch of freshly ground black pepper
Toss the eggplant in the marinade. Grill for 12 to 15 minutes, turning once.

MUSTARD GREENS

1 Tablespoon olive oil

1 cup roughly chopped yellow
    onion

1 Tablespoon minced garlic

3/4 cup finely diced country ham,
    from packaged slices or small
    pieces from a whole ham

16 cups of washed, stemmed
    and roughly chopped mustard
    greens (1 large bundle)

1/2 cup chicken broth

white pepper to taste

It is essential to wash fresh, locally grown mustard greens several times with cold water because they are usually covered with a very fine sand which is not visible to the eye or easy to detect by touch. If you use a deep sink of water, the greens will float to the top and the sand will fall to the bottom.

6 servings

Heat the olive oil in a large stockpot over medium heat Add the onion and garlic and sauté, stirring, for 2 minutes or until the onions are translucent. Add the diced country ham and sauté for 3 minutes, stirring frequently. Gradually add the mustard greens. Cook the greens over medium heat, stirring occasionally until they are all wilted. As they wilt, you will have enough room to get them all into the pot. Add the chicken broth. Cook for 10 minutes, or until the greens are tender but still have a good dark green color. Season to taste with white pepper.

THREE GREENS

Created by Magnolias Chef Don Drake for the 1994 Magnolias James Beard Dinner, this dish was a great surprise: three different greens with three different flavors and textures combined to make a real winner.

6 servings

Heat the olive oil in a large, heavy-bottomed stock pot over medium heat. Add the onions and garlic and sauté for 2 to 3 minutes, stirring, or until the onions are translucent. Add the vinegar and 3 cups of the chicken broth. Add the collards and cook them for 30 minutes, stirring occasionally. Add the remaining 3 cups of chicken broth and the mustard greens and simmer for 15 minutes. Add the watercress and cook for 15 minutes. Add the black pepper and season to taste with salt and Tabasco or the hot sauce of your choice.

1 Tablespoon olive oil

1 cup diced yellow onions, cut in $1/2$-inch dice

2 teaspoons minced garlic

3 Tablespoons cider vinegar

6 cups chicken broth

6 cups washed, stemmed and roughly chopped collard greens

6 cups washed, stemmed and roughly chopped mustard greens

4 cups washed and roughly chopped watercress

$1/4$ teaspoon freshly ground black pepper

salt to taste

Tabasco or a hot sauce of your choice

MAGNOLIAS' COLLARD GREENS

12 cups washed, stemmed, and roughly chopped collard greens, (2 large or 3 small bunches)

2 Tablespoons olive oil

1 cup diced yellow onion, cut in $1/4$-inch dice

1 Tablespoon minced garlic

1 smoked ham hock or 2 smoked neck bones

3 Tablespoons cider vinegar

9 cups chicken broth

2 teaspoons Tabasco, or to taste

salt and freshly ground black pepper to taste

I never had any collard greens until I was introduced to this New Year's Day tradition by my Mother-in-law, Nancy Smith. I found that cooking them long and slow in chicken broth made them better flavored and more silky in texture. The smoked ham hock or neck bones add a subtle smoky flavor.

4 servings

Wash the collard greens very thoroughly with cold water, remove the center stem and the large ribs and give them a rough chop. They should still be leafy. Heat the olive oil in a large heavy-bottomed stockpot over medium heat. Add the onion and garlic and sauté for 2–3 minutes, stirring, or until the onions are translucent. Add the ham hock or neck bones. Add the vinegar and gradually add the collard greens. Cook the greens over medium heat, stirring occasionally, until they are all wilted. As they wilt you will have enough room to get them all into the pot. Add the chicken broth. Add 1 teaspoon of Tabasco. Bring to a boil and simmer for 1 hour and 45 minutes to 2 hours, adding more chicken broth if necessary, one cup at a time, until the greens have a good flavor and are silky in texture.

Add the other teaspoon of Tabasco and salt and pepper to taste.

SPINACH WITH ROASTED GARLIC

The roasted garlic in this dish provides a mild garlic flavor. If you want to use raw garlic, only use a fraction of the roasted quantity and sauté it for a minute longer.

4 to 6 servings

Heat the olive oil in a large heavy-bottomed pan over medium heat. Add the garlic and sauté for 1 minute, stirring. Add one half of the spinach and let it cook until it wilts enough to have room in the pan to add the rest of the spinach. Cook for 2 minutes, or until all of the spinach is wilted. Season to taste with salt and freshly ground black pepper.

Serve at once.

2 Tablespoons olive oil

2 Tablespoons roasted garlic or 1 teaspoon minced fresh garlic (see p. 13)

2 pounds fresh spinach, washed well and stemmed

salt and freshly ground black pepper

BUTTER BEANS

2 Tablespoons butter

1/2 cup diced onions, cut into 1/4-inch dice

1 teaspoon minced garlic

4 cups fresh butter beans (about 1 1/2 to 2 pounds)

6 cups chicken broth

1/4 teaspoon freshly ground black pepper

1 smoked neck bone (optional)

When freshly picked and shelled, these butter beans can almost be a meal in themselves. The chicken stock gives them a unique additional flavor.

4 servings

Heat the butter in a large, heavy bottomed saucepan over medium heat. Add the onions and garlic and sauté, stirring for 2 to 3 minutes, or until the onions are translucent. Add the butter beans and chicken broth. Bring this to a simmer over medium heat, skimming off the foam as it appears.

For a side dish of butter beans, cook them uncovered for a total time of 50 to 55 minutes. Remove the neck bone. The broth will have reduced to 1 cup or so. Lower the heat and break up some of the beans with a whisk or spoon until the remainder of the broth is thickened by the bean starch.

The cooking time for the butter beans in the following recipe for "Succotash" is approximately 20 minutes, or until the beans are just tender but still whole. Remove from the heat and let cool.

If you have to use frozen beans, your cooking time will be reduced because they have been blanched before they were frozen. The cooking procedure will be the same, but use 2 cups less of chicken broth and reduce the cooking time by 25 minutes.

SUCCOTASH

This dish came from Magnolias Chef Casey Taylor's Tennessee roots. The combination of shrimp and vegetables makes an excellent accompaniment to grilled fish or chicken. The Chicken Gravy gives it depth and helps to bring the flavors together.

4 servings

Heat the olive oil in a heavy-bottomed saucepan over medium heat. Add the onions, garlic, red peppers and corn and sauté, stirring for 2 to 3 minutes, or until the onions become translucent. Add the butter beans and mix well. Add the shrimp, spinach, Chicken Gravy and chicken broth. Simmer, stirring, until the shrimp are pink and have begun to curl up.

Season with salt and freshly ground black pepper to taste. Serve immediately.

1 Teaspoon olive oil

1/2 cup diced red onion, cut into 1/2-inch dice

1 teaspoon minced garlic

1/2 cup diced red peppers, cut into 1/2-inch dice

1 1/2 cups cooked fresh yellow corn kernels (see p. 67)

2 cups cooked butter beans (see p. 50)

20 large peeled and deveined shrimp

2 cups washed, stemmed and julienned fresh spinach, cut in 1/4-inch julienne

1 cup Chicken Gravy (see p. 73)

1/2 cup chicken broth

salt and freshly ground black pepper to taste

MAGNOLIAS' GRILLED CHICKEN SALAD WITH CARAMELIZED ONIONS, LEMON VINAIGRETTE AND FRESH PARMESAN OVER MIXED GREENS

For our chicken salad, we slice the breasts diagonally and fan the slices over the mixed greens. We top the chicken with caramelized onions, cooked as in the Pan-Fried Chicken Livers recipe, and dress the salad with the Lemon Herb Vinaigrette, shaved fresh Parmesan, edible herb blossoms and freshly ground pepper to taste. As you can see in the picture on the preceding page, it makes a very hearty and colorful presentation.

4 servings

Combine the soy sauce, olive oil, oregano, thyme, basil, onion powder, garlic powder and black pepper to make a marinade. Toss the chicken breasts with the marinade and refrigerate them for 4 hours or overnight. If necessary, this can be done right before grilling.

Fire your grill.

Place the chicken breasts on a hot grill, close the grill and grill them for 3 to 4 minutes on each side, with the lid down. Remove the breasts and let them rest for a minute before you slice them.

To serve the salads, toss the lettuces lightly with the Lemon Vinaigrette. Mound about 2 cups of lettuces per full size plate. Top each with the slices of chicken and the caramelized onions. Sprinkle with the petals of edible flower blossoms, if desired, shaved curls of fresh Parmesan, and a grind of black pepper.

1 pound of boneless and skinless chicken breasts (about 4 ounces each)

1 teaspoon soy sauce

1 teaspoon olive oil

¼ teaspoon dried oregano

¼ teaspoon dried thyme

¼ teaspoon dried basil

¼ teaspoon onion powder

¼ teaspoon garlic powder

¼ teaspoon freshly ground black pepper

1 pound mixed lettuces, washed and gently dried

1 recipe Caramelized Onions (see p. 26)

Lemon Vinaigrette (see p. 54)

edible flower blossoms if desired

Fresh Parmesan Cheese

MIXED GREENS WITH A LEMON HERB VINAIGRETTE

1–1½ pounds mixed greens, washed well

2 Tablespoons Dijon mustard

2 Tablespoons cider vinegar

¼ cup fresh lemon juice

1 cup olive oil

2 Tablespoons chopped parsley

2 Tablespoons chopped chives

2 Tablespoons finely julienned, then lightly chopped fresh basil

1 teaspoon minced garlic

¼ teaspoon freshly ground black pepper.

This versatile dressing can act as the base of a number of others, as you will see in the two examples below.

Makes 1½ cups, or enough for 8 to 10 salads of mixed lettuce or field greens. I especially like a mixture of red and green oak leaf lettuces, red and green romaines and radicchio.

The emulsion for this dressing can be easily done by mixing the mustard, vinegar and lemon juice in a blender. Turn the blender on low speed and slowly stream in the oil, running the blender for only 30 to 40 seconds. The blender method will give you a creamier, fluffier dressing. After blending, place the vinaigrette in a bowl. Add the herbs, garlic, and black pepper by folding them in with a whisk.

If you are making the dressing by hand, put the mustard, vinegar and lemon juice in a glass, crockery or stainless bowl and whisk them together. Add the olive oil very slowly in a steady stream, whisking vigorously until all the oil is incorporated. Add the herbs, garlic and black pepper by folding them in with the whisk.

Use immediately or store the dressing, covered, in a glass, crockery or stainless steel container in the refrigerator. It should easily keep for a day or two before the ingredients separate. If this does occur, they can simply be remixed before dressing the salads.

LEMON LINGONBERRY VINAIGRETTE

Makes 2¹/₂ cups

Add ¹/₃ cup lingonberry conserve to the Lemon Herb Vinaigrette by folding it in with the herbs. This conserve can be found in specialty shops and on the "gourmet" shelf of most grocery stores.

¹/₃ cup lingonberry conserve

TOMATO HERB VINAIGRETTE

Makes 1³/₄ cups

Take 1 tomato. Cut in half and gently squeeze out the juice and seeds. Dice the flesh. Add to the Lemon Herb Vinaigrette by folding it in with the herbs.

1 tomato

BUTTERMILK, BASIL AND BLUE CHEESE DRESSING

1/4 cup mayonnaise

1/4 cup sour cream

3/4 cup buttermilk

1/4 teaspoon minced garlic

1/4 teaspoon salt

2 Tablespoons honey

2 Tablespoons cider vinegar

1 Tablespoon plus 2 teaspoons julienned fresh basil

1 cup Danish Blue Cheese, Roquefort or Clemson Blue Cheese, crumbled but not mashed

freshly ground black pepper

Low-fat varieties of mayonnaise, sour cream and buttermilk may be used in this recipe. In addition to being a good salad dressing, it also works as a dip for fresh vegetables.

Makes 1³/4 cups or enough for 8 salads of butter lettuce or field greens

Combine the mayonnaise, sour cream, buttermilk, garlic, salt, honey, and vinegar. Whisk lightly to blend until smooth. Fold in the basil and 1/2 cup of the blue cheese. Season to taste with pepper and more salt if desired. After the lettuce is tossed in the dressing and put on salad plates, sprinkle the top of the salads with the remaining 1/2 cup of crumbled blue cheese.

CAROLINA PEANUT VINAIGRETTE

Some peanut oils actually have peanut flavor. Using one of these will enhance this dressing. For heart-smart eating, you may successfully substitute low-fat peanut butter in this recipe. I recommend using the dressing with mixed lettuces, garnished with crushed dry roasted unsalted peanuts and/or crumbled blue cheese.

2 cups dressing or enough for 12-14 salads

Put the peanut butter and the cider vinegar in a glass, crockery or stainless bowl and whisk together to dissolve the peanut butter.

Add the sugar and the garlic. Pour in the peanut oil in a slow steady stream, whisking vigorously to emulsify. Fold in the herbs, and black pepper.

Use immediately or store the dressing, covered, in a glass, crockery or stainless steel container in the refrigerator. It should easily keep for a day or two before the ingredients separate. If this does occur, they can simply be remixed before dressing the salads.

3 Tablespoons creamy or low-fat peanut butter

$1/2$ cup plus 2 Tablespoons cider vinegar

2 Tablespoons light brown sugar

$1^1/2$ teaspoons minced garlic

$1^1/4$ cups peanut oil

2 teaspoons minced parsley

2 teaspoons minced basil

$1/2$ teaspoon freshly ground black pepper

NOTE: You may substitute regular vegetable oil for the peanut oil if you increase the peanut butter by 1 Tablespoon.

MUSTARD SLAW

SLAW DRESSING:

1¹/₂ Tablespoons cider vinegar

¹/₂ cup mayonnaise

1 Tablespoon whole grain
   mustard

1 teaspoon coarse ground black
   pepper

1 teaspoon sugar

SLAW:

6 cups thinly sliced cabbage
   (1 medium cabbage)

1 tightly packed cup grated
   carrot (approximately 2 large
   carrots)

¹/₂ cup slaw dressing

Keeping a couple of the cabbage's dark green outer leaves adds color and texture, making this slaw a little more colorful. It can be made more spicy with a few dashes of hot sauce. We serve Mustard Slaw with our Bar-B-Que Sandwiches and our Grilled Pimiento Cheese Sandwiches.

8 servings

Whisk the cider vinegar into the mayonnaise until smooth. Add the mustard, pepper and sugar and whisk to incorporate. The dressing will keep well for several days in the refrigerator.

Remove the cabbage's tougher outer dark green leaves, but reserve the most tender two or three to use. Wash the cabbage leaves free of all sand and dirt. Julienne the outer leaves. Cut the cabbage in half, remove and discard the white core. Slice thin.

When ready to serve, mix the cabbage, carrot and dressing. Place in the refrigerator for 10 minutes to allow a slight softening of the cabbage.

Mustard Slaw will keep in the refrigerator for 24 hours.

RED POTATO AND PARSLEY SALAD

I prefer to use raw onion in this salad because of my love for this vegetable. For a milder flavor, you could sauté the onions, garlic and parsley in the olive oil, cool and add as directed.

4 servings

Place the potatoes, the Tablespoon of salt and enough water to cover the potatoes together in a heavy bottomed saucepan over medium heat. Bring them to a boil and let them simmer for 8 to 10 minutes. The potatoes should be just fork tender, and not falling apart.

Put ice cubes in a bowl of cold water and set aside. Drain the potatoes. Rinse with cold water and immerse the potatoes in ice water to stop the cooking. When the potatoes are cold, drain them, and place them on paper towels to absorb the excess water.

Combine the parsley, onion, garlic, olive oil and pepper in a medium bowl. Add the potatoes and toss. Add freshly ground black pepper and salt to taste. Serve immediately or refrigerate and serve chilled.

2^1/$_2$ cups diced red potatoes with skin on, cut in about ^{1}/$_2$-inch dice

1 Tablespoon salt

1 Tablespoon finely minced parsley

1 Tablespoon very finely minced yellow onion

1 Tablespoon very finely minced garlic, mashed to a paste

2 Tablespoons extra virgin olive oil

freshly ground black pepper

salt to taste

GRITS, GRAVIES
AND SOUPS

GRITS, GRAVIES AND SOUPS

The highlight of many childhood visits to my grandparents' home was my grandmother's cooking. My favorite dish was her creamy tomato soup. It was nothing more than her own canned tomatoes, roughly chopped, heated with a little milk and finished with salt and pepper. That soup was the inspiration for Magnolias' popular Creamy Tomato Bisque with Lump Crabmeat and a Chiffonade of Fresh Basil.

When I was growing up in West Virginia, grits were not a big item, however hominy was. It was my introduction to this versatile Southern staple. It was also at the top of my list of favorite foods from my grandmother's kitchen, simply served with butter and black pepper. Hominy is a whole kernel form of corn, rather than the ground dried corn which is referred to as grits. Unlike hominy, which can usually be found in a can, pure stone-ground grits aren't found in most grocery stores. Grits may be ordered from mills where the dried corn is still handled today as it was years ago. If you purchase these stone-ground grits, store them in your freezer to keep them fresh.

I don't need to discuss the historical importance of grits in Southern cuisine; Bill Neal and others have already taken care of that. What I will join them in saying is that most people who think that they could never like grits haven't eaten a well cooked dish of the fresh stone-ground product. The grits dishes in this chapter have been among our most popular since the day that Magnolias opened the door to our first customer.

As you prepare the grits recipes, you'll find that all grits react differently to liquid; some will absorb more liquid than others. Stone-ground grits require a longer cooking time and frequent stirring so that they won't settle to the bottom of the pot and burn. The combination of grits cooked with chicken broth and milk or cream makes for a full, rich taste, but do that first long stretch of the cooking using the chicken broth; it doesn't scorch like a dairy product will. The milk or cream can be added to finish the dish. Freshly grated Parmesan, yellow or white cheddar cheeses make interesting flavor additions.

Because grits are so easily scorched, it is appropriate in this chapter of Grits, Gravies and Soups that I explain why I always suggest cooking in heavy-bottomed pans. They distribute the heat evenly, making it less direct and thus reducing the chance of scorching or burning your culinary challenges. Actually, for every type of cooking, the use of heavy-bottomed pans is the equivalent of having an insurance policy for cooking. Another helpful feature to look for in cookware is all-metal construction. The lack of a wooden handle or plastic knob would make a pan oven-proof and able to go directly from burner to oven. Not only is this more convenient, but it saves you time spent over the sink. For any serious cook, I suggest purchasing a stainless steel or aluminum set of cookware. A professional set like this will last a lifetime.

A word about gravies. What makes a "gravy" different from a sauce? I think that most Southerners would say that a gravy is something quickly made—usually from the drippings and juices of a meat thickened with a little flour and maybe finished with cream or milk. I list as gravies: Chicken Gravy, Red-Eye Gravy and Tasso Gravy. The Red-Eye is a perfect example of the simplest of gravies, long considered a fast finish for the morning grits: after you've fried up the sliced country ham, you just deglaze the skillet with black coffee—or Coca-Cola if you happen to live in Georgia.

Magnolias' gravies are only a bit more complex. The Chicken Gravy is actually a simple Velouté sauce, that itself a staple of classic cuisine. The Tasso Gravy is from that same family, enriched by browning chopped Tasso before making the Velouté. But our Red-Eye combines the best of the old and the new.

We can't leave this chapter without talking about another ingredient that I use in a lot of my recipes: Tasso. Tasso is a Cajun pork product that is cured, smoked and then heavily coated with the spicy rub in which it is packed. I became a fan of Tasso many years ago and use quite a bit of it at Magnolias. It is available in specialty stores and can be ordered by mail. I recommend that you make an effort to order some. It has a good shelf life in the refrigerator and freezes very well. If you're ready to cook and don't have time to order Tasso, use my suggested substitution of country ham and Magnolias' Blackening Spice. Use $1/2$ cup of cooked country ham cut in 1 inch strips and 1 Tablespoon of Magnolias' Blackening Spice. This spice mixture pops up in a few recipes in this book, so you may want to keep some on hand.

Grits	Grits	Tasso
Falls Mill	Morgan Mill	K-Paul's La. Mail Order
134 Falls Mills Road	Route 2, Box 395	P. O. Box 23342
Belvidere, TN 37306	Brevard, N.C. 28712	New Orleans, LA 70183
(615) 469-7161	(704) 862-4084	1-800-457-2857

MAGNOLIAS' BLACKENING SPICE

1/2 cup paprika

1 Tablespoon chili powder

2 Tablespoons garlic powder

1 Tablespoon onion powder

1 Tablespoon dried oregano

1 Tablespoon dried basil

1 Tablespoon dried thyme

1 Tablespoon flour

1 Tablespoon cumin

1 Tablespoon salt

1 teaspoon black pepper

1/2 teaspoon cayenne pepper

Makes 1 1/4 cups

Mix all of the ingredients together and store in an air-tight container or a zip lock bag. Spices lose their flavor when they age, so I recommend that you keep the Blackening Spice for no longer than six months.

TO PEEL FRESH TOMATOES

Let this easy method for peeling tomatoes encourage you to use the vine-ripe summer ones when they are in season.

Bring a sauce pot of water to a boil. Put ice cubes in a bowl of cold water and set aside. Core the tomatoes and score their skins lightly with a knife. Immerse the tomatoes in boiling water for 20 to 30 seconds, or until the skin begins to pull back. With a slotted spoon or strainer, remove the tomatoes from the boiling water and immerse in the ice water. When cold, remove the tomatoes from the ice water and peel off the skin. Cut the tomatoes in half. Remove the seeds. Roughly chop the flesh and reserve.

If it's the dead of winter, and there's not a vine-ripened tomato to be had, it's better to use a good quality canned tomato than a pink, tasteless one.

TO PREPARE CANNED PEELED TOMATOES:
Drain the tomatoes. Remove the seeds. Roughly chop the flesh and reserve it with its juice.

SKILLET-SEARED YELLOW GRITS CAKES WITH TASSO GRAVY AND YELLOW CORN RELISH

We refer to this dish, one of our most popular starters, as "Southern Polenta." The trick is to get a good golden crust when pan-frying, while keeping the inside creamy. The Tasso Gravy and Yellow Corn Relish finish the dish off perfectly.

8 Servings

4 cups chicken broth

2¼ cups coarsely ground yellow grits

½ cup heavy cream

salt and white pepper to taste

¾ cup olive oil for frying

coarsely ground cornmeal for dusting

Pour the chicken broth into a heavy-bottomed stockpot or large saucepan and bring it to a boil. Slowly pour in the grits, stirring constantly. Reduce the heat to low and continue to stir so that the grits do not settle to the bottom and scorch. In about 5 minutes, the grits will plump up and become a thick mass. Continue to cook the grits for about 10 minutes, stirring frequently. The grits should have become soft and velvety, but still be firm in consistency. Stir in the heavy cream and cook for another 8 to 10 minutes, stirring frequently. Season to taste with salt and white pepper.

Line a 9"x 9"x 2" pan with waxed paper or spray the pan with non-stick vegetable spray. Pour in the grits and spread them over the bottom of the pan to make them have an even thickness of 1 inch. Let the grits cool in the pan at room temperature, then place the pan into the refrigerator for at least an hour to firm the grits.

Preheat oven to 250 degrees.

When ready to serve the dish, cut the grits into 4 equal 4"x 4" squares. Then cut each square corner to corner to make triangles. Remove the triangles from the pan and lightly dust them with the coarsely ground cornmeal.

Heat 2 Tablespoons of olive oil in a heavy-bottomed skillet over medium heat. Pan-fry the grits cakes, four at a time, turning once, until a golden crust is obtained on both sides. Add olive oil to each pan of grits cakes if the pan is dry. The grits cakes may be

65

held on a baking sheet in the 250 degree oven until all are pan-fried and you are ready to serve them.

TASSO GRAVY

Makes 4 cups

Melt the butter in a heavy bottomed saucepan over low heat. Add the Tasso and sauté for 1 minute, browning slightly. Make a roux by adding the flour and stirring until well combined. Continue to cook over low heat for 5 minutes, stirring very frequently until the roux develops a nutty aroma. Turn the heat up to medium and gradually add 2 cups of the chicken broth, stirring vigorously. Keep stirring constantly until the broth begins to thicken and is smooth. Gradually add the remaining 2 cups of broth and continue to stir as the broth rethickens. Reduce heat and simmer over low heat for 15 minutes to cook out the starchy flavor. Add 1 Tablespoon of the parsley. Simmer for another 5 minutes. Season to taste with salt and white pepper.

When you are ready to serve the grits cakes, place one grits cake on each of 8 warm plates. Spoon the Tasso Gravy over the warm grits cakes and sprinkle with the remaining 1 Tablespoon of parsley. Serve with Fresh Yellow Corn Relish.

YELLOW CORN RELISH

Makes 3 cups

FOR FRESH CORN KERNELS:
Place ice cubes in a bowl of cold water and set aside. Drop the fresh corn on the cob into boiling salted water and cook for 8 minutes. Drain the corn. Rinse with cold water and immerse in ice water to stop the cooking. Drain and pat dry. Cut the kernels off of the cob by slicing with a sharp knife.

FOR CORN RELISH:
Mix all of the ingredients in a bowl and use as needed or put in a storage container with a lid and refrigerate.

TASSO GRAVY:

4 Tablespoons unsalted butter

1/2 cup sliced Tasso, cut into 1 inch strips

1/2 cup flour

4 cups chicken broth

2 Tablespoons finely chopped parsley

salt and white pepper to taste

RELISH:

2 cups fresh yellow corn kernels (about 4 ears)

1/4 cup diced red onion, chopped in 1/4-inch dice

1/2 cup thinly sliced green onion

1 teaspoon chopped garlic

1/4 cup diced red pepper, chopped in 1/4-inch dice

2 teaspoons stemmed, seeded and finely minced jalapeño pepper

1 Tablespoon chopped cilantro

5 Tablespoons extra virgin olive oil

3 Tablespoons cider vinegar

1/2 teaspoon cumin

1/2 teaspoon salt

1/2 teaspoon freshly ground black pepper

GRILLED SALMON FILET WITH DILL BUTTER OVER CREAMY WHITE GRITS

8 servings

DILL BUTTER:

¹/₂ pound unsalted butter, room temperature

1 Tablespoon minced yellow onion

2 Tablespoons chopped fresh dill, or 1 Tablespoon dried dill weed

¹/₄ teaspoon salt

¹/₂ teaspoon freshly ground black pepper

DILL BUTTER:

I prefer to use fresh dill in this recipe. Dried dill weed can't really provide the same sweet taste.

Cream together the soft butter, onion, dill, salt and pepper with a spoon just enough to combine. You may place the mixture in a small bowl, cover with plastic wrap and refrigerate to store. To serve, remove from the refrigerator and let sit at room temperature until soft enough to be easily spooned on top of grilled salmon or any other grilled favorite.

This compound butter can also be rolled up into a log with plastic wrap and refrigerated until cold and firm. It can then be sliced into medallions and placed on top of the hot grilled item.

CREAMY WHITE GRITS:

12 cups chicken broth

4¹/₂ cups coarse stone-ground white grits

1 cup heavy cream

salt and white pepper to taste

CREAMY WHITE GRITS:

Bring the chicken broth to a boil in a heavy bottomed stockpot or large saucepan. Slowly pour in the grits, stirring constantly. Reduce the heat to low and continue to stir so that the grits do not settle to the bottom and scorch. In about 5 minutes, the grits will plump up and become a thick mass.

Continue to cook the grits for about 20–25 minutes, stirring frequently. The grits should have absorbed all of the chicken stock and become soft. Stir in the heavy cream and cook for another 10 minutes, stirring frequently. The grits should have a thick consistency and be creamy like oatmeal.

Season to taste with salt and white pepper. Keep warm over low heat until ready to serve. If the grits become too thick, add warm chicken broth or water to thin them down.

GRILLED SALMON:

Fire the grill.

Season the salmon filets with salt and pepper and brush them with olive oil. Place on the grill with the skin side up. You can recognize the skin side of the filet by its silvery sheen. Any dark meat would also be on the skin side. Grill the filets for 3 to 4 minutes per side until they are firm and flake easily when pierced with a fork.

Fill 4 warm bowls with the Creamy Grits. Place a salmon filet on top of each bowl of grits. Place a spoonful of Dill Butter on top of each filet and let it melt slightly. Serve immediately.

THE GRILLED SALMON:

8 salmon filets, approximately 4 ounces each

salt and freshly ground black pepper

2 Tablespoons olive oil

MAGNOLIAS' SPICY SHRIMP, SAUSAGE AND TASSO GRAVY OVER CREAMY WHITE GRITS

CREAMY WHITE GRITS:

12 cups chicken broth

4½ cups coarse stone-ground white grits

1 cup heavy cream

salt and white pepper to taste

TASSO GRAVY:

4 Tablespoons butter

½ cup sliced Tasso, cut in 1 inch strips

½ cup flour

4 cups chicken broth

2 Tablespoons finely chopped parsley

salt and white pepper to taste

SHRIMP AND SAUSAGE:

½ pound spicy Italian sausage (¾ pound of raw)

1 Tablespoon olive oil

2 pounds medium or large peeled and deveined shrimp

1½ cups chicken broth

1 recipe Tasso Gravy

2 Tablespoons finely chopped parsley

This very popular dish brings together all of the flavors of the Old South. The stone-ground grits are a must. It's a great Lowcountry dish which can be served year round and turns up on local tables morning, noon and night.

8 servings

CREAMY WHITE GRITS:

Bring the chicken broth to a boil in a heavy-bottomed stockpot or large saucepan. Slowly pour in the grits, stirring constantly. Reduce the heat to low and continue to stir so that the grits do not settle to the bottom and scorch. In about 5 minutes, the grits will plump up and become a thick mass.

Continue to cook the grits for about 20–25 minutes, stirring frequently. The grits should have absorbed all of the chicken stock and become soft. Stir in heavy cream and cook for another 10 minutes, stirring frequently. The grits should have a thick consistency and be creamy like oatmeal. Season to taste with salt and white pepper. Keep warm over low heat until ready to serve. If the grits become too thick, add warm chicken broth or water to thin them down.

TASSO GRAVY:

Melt the butter in a heavy-bottomed saucepan over low heat. Add the Tasso. Sauté for 1 minute, browning slightly. Make a roux by adding the flour and stirring until well combined.

(continued on page 72)

Continue to cook over low heat for 5 minutes, stirring frequently until the roux develops a nutty aroma. Turn the heat up to medium and gradually add 2 cups of the chicken broth, stirring vigorously. Keep stirring constantly until the broth begins to thicken and is smooth. Gradually add the remaining 2 cups of broth, stirring constantly until the broth thickens into gravy. Reduce the heat and simmer over low heat for 15 minutes to cook out the starchy flavor. Add the parsley. Simmer for another 5 minutes. Season to taste with salt and white pepper.

SHRIMP AND SAUSAGE:

Preheat oven to 400 degrees.

TO COOK ITALIAN SAUSAGE: Place the Italian sausage on a baking sheet with raised sides. Place on the top rack of the 400 degree oven and bake for 10 to 15 minutes or until the sausage is firm and its juices run clear. Cool and cut into small bite-size pieces.

Heat the olive oil in a heavy-bottomed frying pan over medium heat. Add the precooked sausage and sauté for 2 minutes to brown slightly. Add the shrimp and sauté until they begin to turn pink–no longer than 1 minute. Add 1 cup of the chicken broth to deglaze the pan. Add the Tasso Gravy and one Tablespoon of the parsley. Bring up to a boil and let simmer for 1 minute. The last $1/2$ cup of chicken stock is to be used to thin the gravy if needed.

Divide the hot grits between 8 warm bowls. Spoon the shrimp, sausage mixture over the grits. Sprinkle with the remaining Tablespoon of parsley and serve immediately.

NOTE: If using large shrimp, allow 6 per person; for medium sized shrimp, 8 to 10 shrimp.

CHICKEN GRAVY

This very basic Velouté Sauce makes a great enrichment to simple sauces such as the Red-Eye Gravy. If you have pan drippings, adding them will spark the flavor and deepen the color of the gravy. In the Southern kitchen, Chicken Gravy is served with Fried Chicken and Mashed Potatoes, or just plain over hot biscuits for breakfast.

4 Tablespoons butter

$1/2$ cup flour

4 cups chicken broth

2 Tablespoons finely chopped parsley

salt and white pepper to taste

Melt the butter in a heavy-bottomed saucepan over low heat. Make a roux by adding the flour and stirring until well combined. Continue to cook over low heat for 5 minutes, stirring very frequently until the roux develops a light golden color and has a nutty aroma.

Turn the heat up to medium and gradually add 2 cups of the chicken broth, stirring vigorously. Keep stirring constantly until the broth begins to thicken and is smooth. Gradually add the remaining 2 cups of broth, stirring constantly until the broth thickens into a gravy. Continue to simmer over low heat for 15 minutes to cook out the starchy flavor. Add the chopped parsley and any pan drippings. Season to taste with salt and pepper.

Serve immediately.

RED-EYE GRAVY

1 teaspoon olive oil

1/4 cup chopped country ham

2 Tablespoons finely minced
    yellow onion

1/2 teaspoon minced garlic

1/2 cup strong black coffee

2 Tablespoons unsalted butter

1/4 cup flour

2 cups chicken broth

salt and freshly ground black
    pepper to taste

NOTE: Sliced country ham is available in the butcher's case in most supermarkets. It is packaged like bacon and usually has 4 or 5 thin slices.

This old-fashioned gravy is made a little more interesting by the addition of Chicken Gravy, which mellows its somewhat salty bite.

Makes 2 cups

Heat the olive oil in a heavy-bottomed pan over medium heat. Add the ham and sauté, stirring, for 2 minutes or until the bottom of the pan begins to turn golden and the ham browns. Add the onion and garlic and sauté, stirring, for another 2 minutes. Add the coffee. Deglaze the pan, scraping up all the bits of ham, onion and garlic, as well as the browned juices. Let the coffee cook dry, then add the butter. Make a roux by adding the flour to the melted butter and stirring until well combined. Continue to cook over low heat for 5 minutes, stirring very frequently until the roux develops a light golden color and has a nutty aroma.

Turn the heat up to medium and gradually add 1 cup of the chicken broth, stirring vigorously. Keep stirring constantly until the broth begins to thicken and is smooth. Add the remaining cup of broth, stirring constantly until the broth thickens into a gravy. Continue to simmer over low heat for 15 minutes to cook out the starchy flavor.

Serve immediately or keep warm without cooking further until ready. Season to taste with salt and pepper. The country ham will probably make adding salt unnecessary.

CAJUN CLAM CHOWDER

Magnolias' chowder is a spicier version of the New England clam chowder. You may also add a few leaves of fresh cilantro and a couple of dashes of hot sauce for a nice bang.

12 10-ounce servings

In a heavy-bottomed stock pot over medium heat, render the fat from the chopped bacon without browning the bacon. Add the onions, garlic, jalapeño and Tasso. Sauté over medium heat for 2 to 3 minutes, or until the onions are translucent. Add the olive oil. Make a roux by adding the flour and stirring until well combined. Continue to cook over low heat for 5 minutes, stirring very frequently.

Turn the heat up to medium and add the reserved clam juice and the 3 cups of clam juice or chicken broth, one third at a time, stirring vigorously. With each addition of liquid, it is important to keep stirring constantly until the mixture thickens and is smooth. When all of the liquid is added, reboil and add the diced potatoes and Blackening Spice. Reduce the heat and simmer over low heat for about 30 minutes or until the potatoes are tender. Stir the potatoes frequently while cooking so that they do not settle to the bottom of the pot and scorch. Add the strained clams and the heavy cream. Stir to combine and cook over low heat for another 1 to 2 minutes or until the chowder is hot through. Season to taste with salt, white pepper and cayenne pepper. Garnish with fresh chives.

NOTE: The finished chowder isn't designed to be extremely thick. It should be creamy and just thick enough to coat a spoon.

½ cup chopped smoked bacon (about 4–5 slices)

1 cup diced yellow onion, cut in ¼-inch dice

1 Tablespoon minced garlic

2 Tablespoons stemmed minced jalapeño pepper

½ cup finely chopped Tasso ham

6 Tablespoons olive oil

1 cup flour

3 cups chopped clams, drained, but reserving the juice, (6 10 ½-ounce cans)

3 cups clam juice, or chicken stock if clam juice is not available

3 cups chopped baking potatoes, peeled and cut in ½-inch dice, (about 4 potatoes)

2 teaspoons Magnolias' Blackening Spice (see p. 64)

1 cup heavy cream

salt, white pepper and cayenne pepper to taste

½ cup chopped chives

CREAMY TOMATO BISQUE WITH LUMP CRABMEAT AND A CHIFFONADE OF FRESH BASIL

1/4 cup plus 1 teaspoon extra virgin olive oil

1/2 cup chopped yellow onion

1 teaspoon chopped garlic

1/2 cup flour

3 cups chicken broth

1 chicken bouillon cube

4 cups homemade tomato sauce, or 2 14 1/2-ounce cans of tomato sauce

2 cups tomato juice

3 large peeled fresh vine ripened tomatoes, or 1 14 1/2-ounce can whole peeled tomatoes, crushed with juice (see p. 64)

3/4 cup thinly sliced fresh basil, loosely packed

1 cup heavy cream

1/2 teaspoon salt

dash of white pepper

8 ounces fresh lump crabmeat, picked clean of all shell

Inspired by my grandparents, Buell and Naomi Barickman, with their garden-fresh tomatoes, this soup has been everyone's favorite. The chunky tomatoes, fresh basil and sweet crabmeat make a winning combination.

8 10-ounce servings

Heat the olive oil over medium heat in a heavy-bottomed stockpot. Add the chopped onion and garlic. Sauté for 2 to 3 minutes, stirring, until the onions are translucent. Reduce the heat and make a roux by adding in the flour and stirring until well combined. Continue to cook over low heat for 5 minutes, stirring constantly. Turn the heat up to medium and add 1 1/2 cups of the chicken broth, stirring vigorously. Keep stirring constantly until the broth begins to thicken and is smooth. Gradually add the remaining 1 1/2 cups of chicken broth and the bouillon cube, stirring constantly until the broth rethickens. Reduce heat to low and simmer for 5 minutes to cook out the starchy flavor.

Add the tomato sauce, tomato juice, chopped tomatoes and 1/2 cup sliced basil. Simmer for 10 minutes. Skim off any foam that may collect on the top. Add the heavy cream. Bring to a simmer and skim again if necessary. Taste and add the salt and pepper if desired. When ready to serve, warm the soup bowls. Divide the hot soup mixture between the 8 bowls. Garnish by sprinkling the crabmeat and the remaining 1/4 cup basil over the soup. Serve at once.

FOR THE BLACK BEANS:

4 cups dried black beans (or 5 15-ounce cans, drained but not rinsed)

1 gallon water

6 chicken bouillon cubes

1 teaspoon salt

FOR THE CHILI:

1/4 cup olive oil

4 cups roughly chopped yellow onion

4 Tablespoons minced garlic

4 Tablespoons peeled and minced fresh ginger

2 Tablespoons jalapeño pepper, stemmed and minced

5 cups chicken broth

2 smoked neck bones

6 ounces tomato paste

1 teaspoon freshly ground black pepper

1 Tablespoon cumin

FOR THE PORK:

5 pound pork shoulder or Boston Butt, trimmed of all fat and sinew, or well trimmed and coarsely ground by the butcher

1 Tablespoon olive oil

1 Tablespoon minced garlic

2 Tablespoons freshly ground black pepper

BLACK BEAN CHILI WITH SCALLION AND CILANTRO SOUR CREAM

This award-winning chili took first place when Frank Strauss and I made it for the 1991 South Carolina Chili Cook-Off. It was featured on Magnolias' first menu. Its unique ginger flavor and beany broth with chunks of pork make it a hearty and satifying main course.

Makes 1 gallon

Measure the black beans and pour them out onto a cookie sheet. Pick through them to look for small pebbles and discolored beans. Put the beans in a colander and rinse.

Using a heavy-bottomed saucepan, combine the beans, water, chicken bouillon cubes and salt. Bring to a boil. Reduce to a simmer and cook for about 2 hours or until the beans are very soft but before their skins start to break. Add additional water if needed, a cup at a time. Strain the beans over a large pot or bowl to catch the juice and reserve the juice for use in Black Rice.

Preheat oven to 450 degrees.

Once the beans are cooking, cut the pork shoulder into 1/2-inch dice or smaller, removing as much fat and sinew as possible, or have a butcher coarsely grind it. Lightly toss the pork with the 1 Tablespoon olive oil, 1 Tablespoon minced garlic and 2 Tablespoons black pepper. Spread the pork out onto 2 baking sheets with raised edges to hold in the juices. Roast the pork for approximately 1 hour, or until the meat is nicely browned, but not black. Remove the meat and save all of the juices and brown bits on the baking sheets. When the pork is cool, break it into the diced pieces again and reserve.

Heat the 1/4 cup of olive oil in a heavy-bottomed pot over medium heat. Add the onions, 4 Tablespoons of garlic, 4 Tablespoons of ginger and the jalapeno and sauté, stirring for 2 to 3 minutes, until the onions are translucent. Add the browned

78

pork, chicken broth, neck bones and the tomato paste and the reserved juices from the pork. Let the pork and vegetables simmer over low heat for 40 minutes, or until the pork is quite tender, but not stringy. Add the cooked black beans, black pepper and cumin.

Continue to cook for 10 to 15 minutes over low heat until the flavors join and the consistency of chili is reached. Remove the neck bones.

5 minutes before you are ready to serve the chili, add the cilantro, 1 Tablespoon ginger and the second teaspoon of black pepper and continue to cook over low heat to enhance with fresh flavors.

Pour the chili into warm soup bowls and add a dollop of the Scallion and Cilantro Sour Cream on top of each bowl. Corn Bread makes a great accompaniment.

SCALLION AND CILANTRO SOUR CREAM

Combine the sour cream, scallions, red pepper, garlic, cilantro, cumin, salt and black pepper. Mix well. Serve at once or place in a covered storage container and refrigerate.

FINISH WITH:

2 Tablespoons chopped cilantro

1 Tablespoon minced fresh ginger

1 teaspoon freshly ground black pepper

SCALLION AND CILANTRO SOUR CREAM:

1 cup sour cream

2 Tablespoons minced scallions

1 Tablespoon minced red pepper

1/2 teaspoon minced garlic

1 Tablespoon chopped cilantro

1/2 teaspoon cumin

1/2 teaspoon salt

1/4 teaspoon freshly ground black pepper

FISH AND SHELLFISH

FISH AND SHELLFISH

We are blessed on the South Carolina coast with an abundance of first rate tuna, Black Grouper and dolphin caught only a few miles off of our shores. Our blue crabs, locally farmed clams and catfish are unequaled. When visitors come to Magnolias, they zero in on the opportunity to dine from our local waters.

When selecting and preparing seafood, don't cut quality and don't underestimate the importance of understanding the cooking technique. As for the stocks: fish stock is quite simple. However, the principles of reduction do not apply to fish stock as they do to other stocks. The reduction of fish stock may result in a darker and somewhat overpowering product. My advice is either to freeze it as is, or to make it as needed. I think that this chapter introduction is the place to put the recipes for both fish stock and for the Fish Velouté. Having these in hand will give you everything that you need to meet the challenges of the fish and shellfish recipes.

I think that it's nice to have a couple of quick and easy recipes handy to accompany a fine platter of crabs or batch of fried shrimp. The following recipes fit the bill. I use the Honey Mustard Dip with the Fried Soft Shell Crabs. The Salt and Pepper Shrimp taste especially good with the Honey Mustard and Horseradish Dip.

HONEY MUSTARD AND HORSERADISH DIP

1¹/₂ cups honey

3 Tablespoons whole grain mustard

3 Tablespoons prepared horseradish, squeezed dry in a clean tea towel

1¹/₂ teaspoons chopped parsley

Makes 1³/₄ cups

Combine the honey, mustard, horseradish and parsley and mix well. Serve at room temperature or store in a covered container in the refrigerator for 2 to 3 weeks.

HONEY MUSTARD DIP

¹/₂ cup honey

1 cup Dijon mustard

1 teaspoon chopped parsley

Makes 1¹/₂ cups

Combine the honey, mustard and parsley and mix well. Use at once or pour into a storage container and refrigerate.

FISH STOCK

The real secret to a good fish stock, as in so much of all cooking, comes from using absolutely fresh ingredients. You'll just have to develop a good relationship with your local fish market to ensure a top quality, fresh product.

When preparing the fish carcasses to be used in stock, remove any entrails and rinse out any blood with cold water. If you must include the heads, it is important to remove and discard the gills. Rinse the heads thoroughly as well.

Heat the olive oil in a heavy-bottomed stockpot over medium heat. Add the onions, celery and garlic and sauté for 3 minutes, stirring occasionally. Do not allow this mixture to brown. Add the vermouth and fish bones. Cook for 3 minutes, stirring occasionally. Add the water, thyme, bay leaf, peppercorns and parsley stems. Bring the mixture to a boil, skim off any foam that may appear, reduce to a simmer and cook for 30 to 40 minutes. Longer cooking will only result in an undesirable color and flavor. Strain off the stock and discard the rest.

Store the fish stock in the refrigerator, preferably in a clear container in order to differentiate the stock from the sediment of proteins which will gradually settle to the bottom. Pour slowly in order to separate the clear stock from the sediment. Discard the sediment and use the stock as desired. This stock freezes perfectly.

NOTE: Unlike chicken or veal stock, fish stock usually has only a small amount of oil or fat. If present, it can be removed with a ladle or spoon while the stock is simmering.

2 pounds white fish bones, preferably with no heads included

1 Tablespoon olive oil

1½ cups roughly chopped yellow onions

1½ cups roughly chopped celery stalks, without leaves

⅓ cup roughly chopped garlic cloves

1 cup dry white vermouth

6 cups cold water

2 sprigs fresh thyme or a pinch dry thyme

1 bay leaf

5 cracked black peppercorns

10 parsley stems

FISH VELOUTÉ

2 Tablespoons unsalted butter

$^{1}/_{4}$ cup flour

3 cups of fish stock without sediment

$^{1}/_{2}$ cup heavy cream

$^{1}/_{2}$ teaspoon salt

A Velouté Sauce is a member of a category known as "Mother Sauces" which consist of a combination of fat, flour and a broth or stock, in this case the stock having been made from fish. It serves as the body building source for some of our fish dishes.

In a heavy-bottomed saucepan, melt the butter over low heat without browning. Make a roux by adding the flour and stirring until well combined. Continue to cook over low heat for 5 minutes, stirring very frequently until it has a light golden color and a nutty aroma.

Turn the heat up to medium and add $1^{1}/_{2}$ cups of the fish stock, stirring vigorously. Keep stirring constantly until the sauce begins to thicken and is smooth. Gradually add the remaining $1^{1}/_{2}$ cups of fish stock, stirring constantly until the sauce rethickens and is smooth again. Simmer the sauce for 5 minutes, stirring occasionally. Remove any skin that might form. With the heat on low, continue to simmer for another 10 minutes. You should see bubbles still visibly breaking the surface. Add the $^{1}/_{2}$ cup of heavy cream and simmer for 5 minutes. Add the $^{1}/_{2}$ teaspoon salt.

Remove the sauce from the heat, strain and use immediately or cover, let cool to room temperature, put in a storage container and refrigerate.

OYSTER STEW

Selecting your oysters for flavor and shucking them yourself really makes the difference in this cold weather dish because of the greater flavor and freshness of the oysters.

Note that it is very important not to boil oyster stew, because if you boil it liquid which is released from the oysters will coagulate and cause the stew to loose its silky consistency. When you have reached the right temperature to just curl the oysters, a light steam will be visible, but the stew will not be boiling.

4 servings

Melt the butter in a heavy-bottomed pot over low heat. Add the celery, onion and chives and sauté, stirring, for 2 to 3 minutes, or until the onions are translucent. Add the half and half, pepper, Worcestershire sauce and oysters and stir to incorporate. Heat only until just below the boil, at which point the oysters will begin to curl up. Remove the pot from the heat and serve the stew immediately in warmed soup bowls.

2 Tablespoons lightly salted butter

1/4 cup finely minced celery

1/4 cup finely minced yellow onion

1 Tablespoon chopped chives

4 cups half and half

dash of freshly ground black pepper

1 teaspoon Worcestershire sauce

3 dozen selects in the shell or 1 1/2 pints of oysters, drained of their liquor

SALT AND PEPPER FRIED SHRIMP

2 pounds fresh peeled and deveined medium shrimp

12 cups peanut oil (2 48-ounce bottles)

3 cups flour

1 Tablespoon freshly ground black pepper

1 cup buttermilk

2 teaspoons salt

2 cups flour

1¹/₂ cups fresh dried bread crumbs (see p. 42)

8 servings

Bread the shrimp by using this three-step breading process:

• Combine 1 cup of the flour and 1 teaspoon black pepper. Rinse the shrimp in cold water. Shake off any excess liquid. While the shrimp are still damp, toss them in the flour. Coat the shrimp entirely, leaving no wet spots.

• Combine the buttermilk and salt. Stir to dissolve the salt. Dip the shrimp in this mixture. Coat them entirely, leaving no dry spots.

• Combine the remaining 2 cups of flour, bread crumbs and the remaining 2 teaspoons of black pepper. Roll the shrimp in the bread crumb mixture. Coat entirely, leaving no wet spots.

Put the peanut oil in a deep fat fryer or deep frying pan. If you are using something smaller, use only enough oil to fill the fryer about three quarters of the way up the sides. Gradually heat the oil to 340 degrees by starting to heat it on medium heat and slowly increasing the heat to medium-high. Never put oil in any frying container and turn the heat on to high.

Put a dozen or so shrimp into the hot oil at a time. Too many shrimp will bring down the temperature of the oil. Try to keep the temperature as close to 330 degrees as possible.

Fry, turning frequently until the shrimp are golden brown and float to the top. If the oil is too hot, the crust will brown before the shrimp cook inside. Remove the shrimp from the oil and place on paper towels to absorb any excess oil. Serve at once with Honey Mustard and Horseradish Dip.

MAGNOLIAS' STEAMED PETITE CLAMS WITH FRESH TOMATOES, WHITE WINE, GARLIC AND BASIL

Although it is quite simple, this dish never fails to bring compliments when we serve it at the restaurant. Mussels may be cooked in the same manner, but in an even shorter time. For this recipe, I would use 2 dozen mussels.

4 servings

Put the clams into a wide pot with a lid. Add the onion, garlic, wine, butter, basil and cayenne pepper to the pan with the clams. Place the pot over medium-high heat and steam for 2 minutes. Add the tomatoes and steam for another 2 minutes, or just until the clams open. The clams will release their juices and create a nice broth which combines with the garlic and tomatoes.

Spoon the clams and the rest of the ingredients into warmed soup bowls and serve at once.

NOTE: Before cooking, scrub either clams or mussels with a brush under cold water. Mussels will need to be debearded. Do this by cutting off the "beard" with a sharp knife. Pulling off the beard will kill the mussel.

4 dozen Littleneck clams

1/4 cup minced yellow onion

2 teaspoons minced garlic

1 cup dry white wine

2 teaspoons unsalted butter

2 Tablespoons chopped fresh basil

dash of cayenne pepper

2 cups seeded and diced tomatoes

THE BATTER:

1/2 cup buttermilk

2 eggs

1 1/2 cups flour

1 1/2 teaspoons non-alum baking powder (see p. 31)

2 Tablespoons sugar

2 teaspoons salt

2 teaspoons freshly ground black pepper

1 teaspoon dried thyme

1 teaspoon dried oregano

1 teaspoon dried basil

10 ounces of beer

1 Tablespoon Worcestershire sauce

8 whole soft shell crabs

salt and freshly ground black pepper

1 cup flour for dusting crabs

olive oil for the hors d'oeuvre

1 recipe of Beer Batter

12 cups of peanut oil or canola oil for frying (2 48-ounce containers)

BUTTERMILK AND BEER BATTER FRIED SOFT SHELL CRABS

This is Nature's way for us to enjoy the whole crab without any fear of handling these little devils and without the painstaking process of picking their sweet white meat from the ever-present shell. There are many ways to serve these delicacies. I've listed three. My personal favorite is the batter-dipped legs and claws. They make an excellent finger food or hors d'oeuvre.

8 servings

THE BATTER:

Beat together the buttermilk and eggs. Combine the flour, baking powder, sugar, salt, black pepper, thyme, oregano and basil. Slowly sprinkle 1/2 of the flour and herb mixture into the buttermilk and egg mixture, whisking it into a smooth paste. Add the remaining 1/2 of the flour and herb mixture and whisk until smooth. Slowly add the beer, whisking until the mixture is smooth. The mixture should be thick and batter-like. Whisk in the Worcestershire sauce.

Put peanut oil or canola oil in a deep fat fryer or deep frying pan. If you are using something smaller, use only enough oil to fill the fryer about three quarters of the way up the sides. Gradually heat the oil to 340 degrees. Start heating it on medium heat and gradually increase the heat to medium high. Never put oil in any frying container and turn the heat to high.

TO CLEAN THE CRABS:

Remove the gills on the left and right sides of the top of the crab by lifting up each side of the shell. These are known as "the dead man's fingers." Remove the reproductive organs located at the bottom of the crab. Peel them back and snip off with scissors. Trim off the face.

TO FRY THE CRABS WHOLE OR SERVE AS AN HORS D'OEUVRE:

Put the peanut oil or canola oil in a deep fat fryer or deep frying pan. If you are using something smaller to fry in, use only enough oil to fill the fryer about three quarters of the way up the sides. Gradually heat the oil to 340 degrees by starting to heat it on medium heat and slowly increasing the heat to medium-high. Never put oil in any frying pan and turn the heat to high.

To fry the crabs whole, you do not have to precook the crabs. Dust the crabs with flour. Shake off any excess. Holding the crabs by their 2 back fins, immerse them in the batter. Then carefully immerse the crabs into the hot oil. Put 2 whole crabs in at a time. They may spit and splatter, so have a splatter guard handy. Try to keep the oil temperature steady at about 340 degrees. Fry the crabs until they are golden brown. Remove the crabs from the oil and place on paper towels for a moment to absorb any excess oil. You may hold the crabs in a 225 degree oven until all are fried. Then serve at once with Honey Mustard Dip. (see p. 82)

TO CUT AND FRY THE CRABS INTO PIECES FOR HORS D'OEUVRE:

Season and flour the crabs. Sauté in hot olive oil for 1 to 2 minutes on each side. Remove the crabs from the pan and refrigerate to cool them quickly. Pull off the claws. Pull off the top shell. Cut the body of the crab down the center. Then cut it across between the 4 legs. You should have 6 pieces per crab: 2 claws and 4 leg pieces.

Working with 12 pieces at a time, use the claw and leg ends as handles and dip the white meat end into flour. Shake off any excess. Then immerse the pieces into the batter. Carefully immerse them into the hot oil. The pieces may spit and splatter, so have a splatter guard handy. Try to keep the oil temperature as close to 340 degrees as possible. Fry the pieces until they are golden brown. Remove the pieces from the oil and place on paper towels for a moment to absorb any excess oil. Serve at once with the Honey Mustard Dip. (see p. 82)

For Spicy Soft Shell Crabs:
Dredge the cleaned crabs in Magnolias' Blackening Spice (see p. 64) and sauté in olive oil over medium-high heat for about 2 minutes on each side.

NOTE: The Beer Batter may also be used for shrimp. It will batter about 3 pounds of peeled and deveined shrimp, tails on.

CRAB AND YELLOW CORN CAKES WITH TOMATO, CORN AND CHIVE BUTTER

1 pound jumbo lump or lump crabmeat

1/4 cup finely minced red onion

1/4 cup finely minced red pepper

1/2 cup cooked fresh yellow corn kernels, chopped fine (1 ear) (see p. 67)

1/2 cup mayonnaise

1/4 cup chopped fresh basil

1 teaspoon salt

1/4 teaspoon white pepper

dash of cayenne pepper

1 3/4 cups fresh Corn Bread crumbs (see p. 34)

olive oil for frying

The use of corn bread crumbs in this recipe makes these crab cakes unique. The other key is to chop the vegetables very fine. Otherwise, the cakes will crumble and break apart. While the size of your budget or the stature of your guests may determine the quality of your crab meat, try to buy the best that you can afford and try to never use frozen.

Makes 12 cakes

Gently pick the lump crab meat over to remove any shell, but do not shred the crab meat or break down the lumps. Gently mix the crab, onion, red pepper, corn kernels, mayonnaise, basil, salt, pepper and cayenne pepper. Add the corn bread crumbs, mix gently and let rest for 5 minutes to moisten the crumbs. Scoop out the mixture with a 1/4 cup measure to make the cakes. Use your hands to gently pat out the cakes.

Heat 1 Tablespoon of olive oil in a non-stick frying pan or a well seasoned sauté pan over medium heat. Pan-fry the crab cakes in two batches, adding more olive oil, 1 teaspoon at a time, if the pan dries as you cook. Sauté the cakes for 3 to 4 minutes on each side until they are golden brown, turning them only once. The crab cakes may be held in a 225 degree oven until all are sautéed.

Spoon Yellow Corn, Tomato and Chive Butter onto warm plates, place 2 crab cakes on each plate and serve immediately.

90

TOMATO, CORN AND CHIVE BUTTER

This sauce requires a bit of reduction and is sensitive to an overly hot or cold temperature once you start to add the butter. It will acquire a nice rose color from the addition of the tomato. It's loaded with fresh corn kernels and will accompany any seafood very well.

Makes 2 cups.

Heat 1 Tablespoon of the butter in a heavy-bottomed sauté pan over medium heat. Sauté the onion and garlic for 2 to 3 minutes or until the onion is translucent. Turn the heat up to medium-high and add the vermouth. Cook, stirring occasionally, until the vermouth is reduced by half.

Add the chicken broth and reduce the liquid by two-thirds. Add the heavy cream and continue to reduce the liquid until it thickens and becomes very bubbly. Add 1 Tablespoon of the chopped tomato and all of the corn. Reduce the heat to low and drop the 12 Tablespoons of butter in one Tablespoon at a time, after each melts, stirring constantly. Try to keep the temperature between 130 and 150 degrees when you are adding the butter. It is very important that the sauce does not boil, or the butter will separate. The butter will also separate if the sauce becomes too cool.

After the butter is incorporated, fold in the rest of the chopped tomatoes and the chives. Season with salt to taste. Serve immediately or hold in a warm area, like on top of the stove but off of the burner, for 30 to 40 minutes. Do not put the chives in until it is the time to serve the sauce because their color will fade.

13 Tablespoons unsalted butter

2 Tablespoons finely minced yellow onion

1 teaspoon finely minced garlic

$1/4$ cup dry vermouth

1 cup chicken broth

2 Tablespoons heavy cream

$1/2$ cup peeled, seeded and finely chopped fresh tomato (about $1/2$ of a tomato) (see p. 64)

1 cup cooked fresh yellow corn kernels (about 2 ears) (see p. 67)

$1/4$ cup chopped chives

salt to taste

PAN-FRIED CATFISH WITH CREOLE SAUCE, COLLARD GREENS AND BLACK RICE

16 boneless, skinless pieces of catfish, approximately 3 ounces each

salt and freshly ground black pepper

stone-ground yellow corn meal

3 Tablespoons olive oil

Creole Sauce (see p. 94)

Collards (see p. 48)

Black Rice (see p. 41)

Anyone who has bottom-fished for catfish will agree that farm-raised fish have a sweeter, fresher flavor. Being blessed with a local catfish farm, we are able to serve catfish that is harvested and fileted each day. That's my choice for Magnolias.

8 servings of 2 catfish filets per person

Season the catfish filets with salt and pepper. Dust with cornmeal. Shake off the excess.

Heat the olive oil in a heavy-bottomed frying pan over medium-high heat. Place the catfish filets in the pan skin side up. You can recognize the skin side of a filet by its silvery sheen. In some fish there is also a dark fatty layer on the skin side.

Shake the pan gently to keep the filets from sticking. Lower the heat to just below medium. Slowly pan-fry the filets until the bottoms turn a light golden brown. Turn the filets over and slowly cook for 5 minutes, or until the flesh flakes easily when pierced with a fork. Add a little more olive oil, a teaspoon at a time, if the pan becomes dry.

Remove the filets from the pan and place on warmed plates. Add servings of Collards and Black Rice. Ladle the Creole Sauce around the edge.

4 Tablespoons olive oil

$3/4$ cup diced red onion, cut into $1/2$-inch dice

$3/4$ cup diced red peppers, cut into $1/2$-inch dice

$3/4$ cup diced green peppers, cut into $1/2$-inch dice

2 Tablespoons minced garlic

1 Tablespoon stemmed and minced jalapeño pepper

$3/4$ cup diced celery

$1 1/2$ cups sliced fresh okra, cut $1/4$-inch thick

$1 1/2$ cups yellow corn kernels (about 2 ears)

1 teaspoon dried basil, or 2 teaspoons fresh basil

1 teaspoon dried thyme, or 2 teaspoons fresh thyme

1 teaspoon dried oregano, or 2 teaspoons fresh oregano

$1/4$ cup plus 2 Tablespoons flour

$3 1/2$ cups chicken broth

3 Tablespoons tomato paste

1 cup peeled, seeded and diced fresh, vine ripened tomato (about 1 tomato)

1 teaspoon worcestershire sauce

1 teaspoon Magnolias' Blackening Spice (see p. 64)

1 teaspoon freshly ground black pepper

salt to taste

CREOLE SAUCE

In Southern cuisine, okra has long been used as a thickening agent through cooking it down, as seen in such dishes as Louisiana gumbo and jambalaya. In our Creole, however, I chose to use a little roux as the thickener because I wanted to keep the fresh integrity of all of the vegetables.

8 servings with Pan-Fried Catfish

Heat the olive oil in a heavy-bottomed stockpot over medium heat. Add the red onion, red and green peppers, garlic, jalapeño, celery, okra and corn. Toss together and sauté for 3 minutes, stirring to prevent scorching. Add the basil, thyme and oregano. Sauté for 2 more minutes. Add the flour and stir well. Stir in the chicken broth and slowly bring the mixture up to a boil, stirring constantly as it thickens. Add the tomato paste and stir to completely dissolve. Add the tomato. Add the Worcestershire, Blackening Spice and black pepper. Season to taste with salt and stir to combine. Simmer for 5 more minutes.

Serve at once or let cool and reheat when ready to serve.

NOTE: If good, flavorful tomatoes are not available, substitute a $14 1/2$ ounce can of whole tomatoes with their juice. However, if you use canned tomatoes, use only $2 1/2$ cups of the chicken broth and only 2 Tablespoons of the tomato paste.

GRILLED GROUPER AND VEGETABLES WITH LEMON AND FRESH HERBS

Grouper is a member of the Sea Bass family which is composed of many species. My favorite is the Black Grouper which inhabits our local waters. I have yet to find a milder or more satisfying tasting fish. It's excellent in this dish because it works well on the grill.

4 servings

Fire your grill.

Cut the eggplant, onion, red pepper and squash into 1/4-inch thick slices. Wash the green onions. Cut off the roots and any yellow tips on the green end. Place the vegetables in a glass or crockery container. Lightly toss with just enough olive oil to coat, the black pepper and the minced garlic. Let the vegetables marinate for 5 minutes at room temperature. Place the vegetables on the hot grill and cook, turning occasionally, until they are tender and cooked through. Watch carefully, because some vegetables will be ready before others. Keep the vegetables warm while grilling the filets.

Brush the grouper filets lightly with olive oil and sprinkle with black pepper. Place them on the grill and cook for 5 to 10 minutes, turning once or twice, until done, or until a fork inserted into the fish easily flakes the flesh.

Warm 4 plates and divide the warm vegetables between them. Place a grilled filet on top of each plate. Garnish with half of a lemon and a good sprinkle of the mixed herbs.

NOTE: The rule of thumb when cooking fish is the Canadian Rule which states that you usually cook fish 10 minutes per inch of thickness. Of course, a very hot or a very cool grill will influence the cooking time.

1 small eggplant

1 large yellow onion, peeled

1 red pepper, cored and seeded

1 yellow summer squash

1 bunch green onions

4 Tablespoons extra virgin olive oil

freshly ground black pepper

1 large garlic clove, minced

4 Black Grouper filets, weighing approximately 5 ounces

2 lemons, halved

4 sprigs each of fresh basil, thyme, parsley and chives, minced and mixed together

SAUTÉED GROUPER WITH CRAYFISH AND YELLOW CORN AND LEEK CREAM

FOR THE SAUCE:

1 Tablespoon olive oil

3 Tablespoons minced yellow onion

1½ teaspoons minced garlic

1 cup cooked fresh yellow corn kernels (see p. 67)

1 cup julienned leeks, cut in 1-inch strips

½ cup dry vermouth

1½ cup Fish Velouté (see p. 84)

½ cup heavy cream

1½ cups cooked crawfish tail meat

1 Tablespoon chopped parsley

½ teaspoon salt or salt to taste

freshly ground black pepper to taste

FOR THE FISH:

2 Tablespoons olive oil

6 black grouper filets, approximately 5 ounces each

salt and freshly ground black pepper

flour for dusting the filets

Although crayfish are now farm-raised in South Carolina, this dish can also be made with lobster, shrimp or crab. When prepared with lobster, this is one of the restaurant's most popular entrées.

6 servings

Heat the olive oil in a heavy-bottomed frying pan over medium heat. Sauté the onion and garlic for 2 to 3 minutes or until the onions are translucent. Add the corn and leeks. Continue to sauté them for ½ minute. Add the ½ cup vermouth. Cook over medium heat until the vermouth reduces by one half. Add the Fish Velouté and cream and cook over medium heat for 2 to 3 minutes longer. Add the crayfish tail meat. Reduce the sauce over medium heat for 2 to 3 minutes, or until it will lightly coat a spoon. Add the parsley, black pepper and salt to taste. Keep the sauce warm while sautéing your fish.

Preheat oven to 325 degrees.

Heat 2 Tablespoons of olive oil in a heavy-bottomed frying pan over medium high heat until the oil is smoking. Season the filets with salt and pepper. Dust with flour. Shake off any excess flour so that it does not burn in the pan. Sauté the filets with the skin side up for 2 to 3 minutes. You can recognize the skin side of a filet by its silvery sheen. Turn when golden.

Remove the frying pan from stove and place it in the 325 degree oven. Bake the filets at 325 for 4 to 5 minutes, or until a fork inserted into the fish easily flakes the flesh. Divide the sauce between 6 warm plates. Remove the grouper from the oven and place the filets on top of the sauce. Serve immediately.

NOTE: If using shelled crayfish, do not rinse them because they come packed in their own roe; the essence of the roe adds color and flavor to the sauce.

PAN-SEARED PEPPERED DOLPHIN SALAD
WITH TOMATO VINAIGRETTE

Pepper-searing an item is an acquired, trained skill. Many people regard black pepper as a mild pepper, but when it is freshly cracked it can create a very spicy heat. Use it in moderation. I grind my black pepper in an electric coffee bean grinder to the desired coarseness.

4 servings

Preheat oven to 350 degrees.

Remove any dark reddish meat from the dolphin filets. Lay them skin side down, brush them with olive oil and sprinkle them with salt and the cracked pepper. You can recognize the skin side of a filet by its silvery sheen.

Heat 2 Tablespoons of olive oil until smoking in a heavy-bottomed sauté pan over medium heat. Gently place the filets in the pan, pepper side down, and sear, without turning, for 2 to 3 minutes or until the pepper side is golden and has a light crust. Turn the filets pepper side up and place them in the 350 degree oven and cook for 3 to 5 minutes until the fish is firm and flakes easily when pierced with a fork.

Wash the Romaine and tear it into small pieces. Spin or pat dry. Divide the lettuce between 4 plates. Remove the fish from the oven and place one filet on each plate of lettuce. Top with Tomato Vinaigrette and serve immediately.

4 skinless filets of dolphin, approximately 4 ounces each

$1/4$ cup olive oil

salt

finely cracked black pepper

1 large head of Romaine lettuce

Tomato Vinaigrette (see p. 55)

FILET OF GRILLED DOLPHIN WITH A SUCCOTASH OF SHRIMP, BUTTER BEANS, YELLOW CORN AND FRESH SPINACH

4 servings

SUCCOTASH:

1 Teaspoon olive oil

1/2 cup diced red onion, cut in 1/2-inch dice

1 teaspoon minced garlic

1/2 cup diced red pepper, cut in 1/2-inch dice

1 1/2 cups cooked fresh yellow corn kernels (see p. 67)

2 cups cooked butter beans (see p. 50)

20 large peeled and deveined shrimp

2 cups washed, stemmed and julienned fresh spinach

1 cup Chicken Gravy (see p. 73)

1/2 cup chicken broth

salt and freshly ground black pepper to taste

DOLPHIN:

4 skinless dolphin filets, 6 to 7 ounces each

1/4 cup olive oil

salt and freshly ground black pepper

Heat the olive oil in a heavy-bottomed saucepan over medium heat. Add the onions, garlic, red peppers and corn and sauté, stirring for 2 to 3 minutes, or until the onions become translucent. Add the butter beans and mix in well. Add the shrimp, spinach, Chicken Gravy and chicken broth. Simmer, stirring until the shrimp are pink and have begun to curl up and the spinach is wilted. Season with salt and freshly ground black pepper to taste.

Fire your grill.

Remove any dark reddish meat from the dolphin filets. Brush them with olive oil and sprinkle with salt and black pepper. Place the filets on the hot grill, skin side up. You can recognize the skin side of the filet by its silvery sheen. Grill the filet for 6 to 7 minutes per side.

Divide the hot Shrimp Succotash between 4 warm plates. Place the grilled dolphin on top and serve immediately.

CRABMEAT STUFFED FLOUNDER SERVED WITH RED POTATO AND PARSLEY SALAD AND A YELLOW CORN COULIS

2 9" by 13" pans

4 pounds of flounder filets, cut into approximately 3 ounce portions, with all bones trimmed out

ice water

salt

freshly ground black pepper

THE FISH MARINADE:

$1/2$ cup dry white table wine, of drinking quality

juice of 1 lemon

1 teaspoon Worcestershire sauce

STUFFING:

1 recipe Crab Dip (see p. 20)

THE POACHING LIQUOR:

2 cups dry white table wine, of drinking quality

2 cups fish stock (see p. 83)

8 Servings, allowing 3 roulades per person

Place the filets on a sheet of plastic wrap. Sprinkle each filet with a little ice water. This will keep the fish moist and keep the plastic wrap from sticking. Cover the filets with a second sheet of plastic wrap. With the flat side of a chef's knife blade or a flat mallet lightly pound the filets out to about $1/2$ again their thickness. This breaks down the fiber of the fish and allows it to cook quickly and evenly.

Lay out the filets, skin side up on a cutting board. You can recognize the skin side of a filet by its silvery sheen.

Preheat oven to 350 degrees.

To make the marinade, combine the $1/2$ cup of white wine with the lemon juice and Worcestershire sauce. Sprinkle the filets with a little salt, black pepper and the marinade. Place 2 Tablespoons of the Crab Dip at one end of each of the filets. Spread it up about $3/4$ of the length of the filets. Roll the filets up, starting from the filled end. Divide the filets between the 2 baking pans. Mix the 2 cups of wine with the 2 cups of fish stock. Divide it between the two pans, pouring it to come about one-third of the way up the sides of the fish roulades. Lightly cover the pans with aluminum wrap, but do not seal the edges so that the steam will be able to escape.

Bake the filets for 20 minutes, or until they are white and opaque. The roulades should be firm and bouncy but still tender and moist. Remove them from the pans and serve at once or, leave in the pans with the poaching liquid and hold in a 250 degree oven for no more than 10 minutes.

Serve with Yellow Corn Coulis and Red Potato and Parsley Salad. (see p. 59)

Garnish with Whole Cooked Corn Kernels (see p. 59).

YELLOW CORN COULIS

Makes 2 cups

Heat the olive oil in a heavy bottomed saucepan over medium heat. Add the onion and garlic and sauté, stirring occasionally, for 2 to 3 minutes, or until the onions are translucent. Do not allow this mixture to brown. Add the chicken broth, cream, raw corn kernels and seasonings. Cook over medium heat, stirring frequently, for 10 to 15 minutes. Remove any foam that might appear. Remove the sauce from the heat and let cool slightly. Purée the sauce in a blender or food processor and strain. Add the $1/8$ teaspoon black pepper. Season with salt to taste. Rewarm and serve, garnished with cooked corn kernels and chopped chives.

1 Tablespoon olive oil

$1/2$ cup finely chopped yellow onion

1 teaspoon minced garlic

$1^1/2$ cups chicken broth

2 cups heavy cream

3 cups fresh raw yellow corn kernels, cut from the cob (about 6 ears)

$1/8$ teaspoon freshly ground black pepper

salt to taste

3 Tablespoons cooked corn kernels for garnish (see p. 67)

2 Tablespoons chopped chives for garnish

MEATS AND POULTRY

MEATS AND POULTRY

Of all of the many areas of restaurant food, it is in the meat and seafood categories that reputations are most easily made or broken. The number one reason is that poor quality will quickly stand out. Actually, when it comes to selecting good quality, Mother Nature does most of the work for us. What's left to the chefs is the challenge of understanding the cuts of meat and types of poultry and matching them with correct ingredients and techniques of preparation. In addition, price is almost always a helpful indicator of the quality of the product.

Learning about the techniques of cooking was the very thing that clinched my decision to study at The Culinary Institute of America. When I looked at the C.I.A.'s brochures, I began to realize that this school was the answer to all of the frustrations I faced when a recipe didn't turn out or when I came across terminology that appeared to be in a different language. It made me realize that there was a lot more to cooking than just following a recipe. There are methods which were developed many years ago which set the foundation of ground rules for cooking today and which must be understood to have a relative idea about what you are doing. I wanted to have all of the answers and I figured out that the quickest way to get them was to go full steam ahead for the best Culinary school in the nation.

Good sauces are based upon technique, as you'll see when you read the recipe for Madiera Sauce. In the Grits, Soups and Gravies chapter I talked about what a "gravy" could be. But there are times when a dish merits a fine sauce. Magnolias' Filet with Madeira Sauce is a perfect example. (And while you're taking the time to make that Madeira Sauce, make a little extra and see what it does for the Pan-Fried Chicken Livers.)

One of the foundations for a great sauce is a flavorful stock or broth. In the case of Madiera Sauce, it is Veal Stock. There are those cooks who have a lot of pride in their cooking and will make their own stock, and I recommend it to anyone who can take the time. But these days there are many people who barely have the time to cook, much less to make stock. There are not really any excellent veal or seafood stocks readily available except through specialty food stores and these are usually quite expensive. It is best that you seek out the ingredients and make your own. However, there is good chicken stock at your fingertips. The manufacturers call it "broth" instead of stock, so I will refer to it this way in the book so that there will be an easy association with it as the product on the supermarket shelf.

When purchasing chicken broth, be sure that you choose one that is low in fat and sodium. In many of these recipes the broth will reduce and concentrate, which could lead to an over-salted product. It's best to season the finished product to taste. I have also used chicken bouillon cubes in some of these recipes to enhance the flavor. These can be very helpful as a seasoning agent to bring out the flavors of the other ingredients, but they carry the same caveat to not add any salt until the recipe is finished.

For those who have the time, here is the Magnolias' recipe for chicken stock/broth. Remember that it can be cooked down and reduced to a concentrate. Freeze this in ice cube trays, and put the cubes into a freezer bag once they are frozen; it takes up much less space and there are no additives.

CHICKEN BROTH

This broth is extensively used throughout the book and in our restaurant. It produces the flavor base for many of my recipes. I don't know how today's chefs could do without it—we use it like water. If only we could have it piped in!

Makes 2¹/₂ quarts

Combine all of the ingredients in a large stockpot and bring them to a boil over high heat. Reduce to a simmer and slowly simmer uncovered for 2¹/₂ hours, skimming off any foam and any excessive amounts of fat which appear on the top. Strain and discard the bones and vegetables.

Store the broth in the refrigerator, preferably in a clear container in order to differentiate the broth from the sediment of proteins which will gradually settle on the bottom. Pour the broth off slowly to separate the clear broth from the sediment. Discard the sediment. When the broth has been chilled, it is easy to remove the fat from it. The fat will rise to the top and you can lift it off with a spoon.

The broth will keep for several days in the refrigerator or for several months in the freezer.

2¹/₂ pounds chicken backs, rinsed with cold water

1¹/₂ cups roughly chopped yellow onion

1 cup roughly chopped carrot (about 2 large carrots)

1 cup roughly chopped celery stalks, but no leaves

4 large cloves of garlic, roughly chopped

2 bay leaves

8 sprigs of fresh thyme, or ¹/₂ teaspoon dried thyme

10 parsley stems

6 cracked peppercorns

16 cups water

PORK BAR-B-QUE SANDWICH WITH MUSTARD SLAW AND SWEET PEPPER RELISH

1 Boston Butt or Picnic Ham
(about 5 pounds)

2-3 Tablespoons of Magnolias'
Blackening Spice (see p. 64)

MOPPING SAUCE:

3 cups cider vinegar

1½ cups brown or Dijon mustard

Obviously, there are many different ways to cook this Southern favorite and many different pieces of equipment that could be used. Here are suggestions for two home methods which can produce a mouth-watering product. The key is to cook slowly over low heat—although not under 200 degrees—with a small amount of smoke.

Makes 2½ pounds

TO GRILL ON A GAS GRILL:

Use oak or hickory chips soaked in water to produce the smoky flavor. Tuck the wet wood down by the burner so that you get smoke and not burning wood.

Rub the pork with the Blackening Spice. Grill for an hour over medium heat. Move the meat to one side of the grill. Turn the flame off of that side so that the fat doesn't drip and flame up. Check about every hour to make sure that you have wood that is producing a light smoke and to baste with the Mopping Sauce. Using a mustard squirt bottle or a baster, put the nozzle up under the fat and also baste there to help break down the fat.

Continue to grill over medium heat for 8 to 10 hours. You want to reach an internal temperature of 190 degrees, at which point the meat is done and tender enough to fall off the bone.

TO COOK IN THE OVEN:

Preheat oven to 350 degrees.

Rub the pork with Blackening Spice. Place the pork in the 350 degree oven and roast for an hour. Lower the temperature to 210 degrees and continue to cook for about 10 hours, basting with Mopping Sauce about every hour. Roast to an internal

temperature of 190 degrees, at which point the meat is done and tender enough to fall off the bone.

NOTE: If you are cooking in the oven, save the juices to put in the Bar-B-Que Sauce, using the following procedure. Pour the grease off and deglaze the pan with a little water. Pour this into a container and put into the refrigerator. When the grease comes to the top and solidifies, remove it and use the pure juice to give more depth and flavor to the "Q" sauce.

BAR-B-QUE SAUCE

1¹/₂ **cups cider vinegar**

¹/₄ **cup Dijon mustard**

1 **cup ketchup**

2 **Tablespoons Worcestershire sauce**

1 **teaspoon freshly ground black pepper**

1 **Tablespoon Tabasco sauce**

¹/₄ **cup black strap molasses**

2 **Tablespoons dark brown sugar**

This is a cross between a mopping sauce and a more traditional Bar-B-Que sauce. It works well with any pork, ribs or chicken. It can be heated and tossed with freshly pulled pork Bar-B-Que or served in a bowl on the side. Add the pan drippings from the roasted pork if you cook your meat in the oven.

Makes 2 cups

Combine all of the ingredients in a heavy-bottomed saucepan over medium heat. Simmer for 5 minutes to meld the flavors. The sauce should be just thick enough to coat a spoon. Use at once or let cool at room temperature, cover and refrigerate. The Bar-B-Que Sauce will keep for about a week in the refrigerator if it has pan drippings in it or several weeks if not.

NOTE: If you desire a less tangy sauce, only use ³/₄ cup of vinegar and add ³/₄ cup chicken broth.

SEARED STRIP STEAK WITH SWEET POTATOES AND MUSHROOMS

Almost any kind of mushroom goes well with steak, but my suggestion for this recipe would be a mixture of shiitake, oyster, portobello and cremini mushrooms.

2 servings

Preheat oven to 400 degrees.

Inspect the steaks to be sure that as much fat is trimmed off as is possible. Rub them with 1 teaspoon of the olive oil, some salt and freshly ground pepper, and set aside.

Toss the sweet potatoes with 2 teaspoons of olive oil and spread them out on a sheet pan. Roast the potatoes in the 400 degree oven for 15 to 20 minutes or until they are light brown on the outside and tender on the inside. Remove them from the oven and let them sit at room temperature until you are ready to use them.

Lower the oven temperature to 350 degrees.

Heat 1 teaspoon of the olive oil in a heavy-bottomed pan over medium-high heat until the oil is smoking. Gently lay the steaks in the pan and allow them to sear for 4 minutes, or until a nicely seared, caramelized crust is obtained. Be careful to lower the heat as needed to prevent the steaks from burning instead of just searing. Turn the steaks over and place the pan in the 350 degree oven for:

- 1 minute for rare
- 2 minutes for medium rare
- 3–4 minutes for medium
- 4–5 minutes for medium well to well done

2 New York Strip Steaks, cut 1-inch thick and about 10 ounces each

2 Tablespoons olive oil

salt

freshly ground black pepper

2 cups peeled, diced sweet potatoes, cut into $1/2$-inch dice (about 2 sweet potatoes)

1 teaspoon minced garlic

$2^1/_2$ cups roughly chopped assorted wild mushrooms (about 3 to 4 ounces)

1 cup chopped green onions, cut in 1-inch segments

1 cup chicken broth

Remove the pan from the oven and place the steaks on a warmed plate. Spoon off any fat remaining in the pan. Add the remaining 2 teaspoons of olive oil and place the pan over medium heat. Add the garlic and stir. Add the mushrooms and sauté for about 2 minutes. The mushrooms should be cooked but still firm. Add the green onions, cooked sweet potatoes and chicken broth. Gently simmer this mixture for 2 minutes or until the liquid volume has reduced by half. Season to taste with salt and freshly ground black pepper.

Place the steaks on their serving plates and spoon the mushroom and sweet potato mixture over them. Drizzle the *jus* over the mushrooms and sweet potato mixture and the steaks and serve immediately.

GRILLED FILET OF BEEF TOPPED WITH PIMIENTO CHEESE AND SERVED WITH GRILLED TOMATOES, GREEN ONIONS, PARSLIED POTATOES AND A MADEIRA SAUCE

As you can see in the picture of this dish, at the restaurant we spoon some of the Madeira Sauce on each warm plate, then add the Grilled Filets, Parslied Potatoes, Grilled Tomatoes and Green Onions. All of these recipes are included in the book. The Pimiento Cheese warms and makes a colorful topping. The combination of flavors, textures and colors makes this an outstanding dish.

4 servings

Fire your grill.

Brush the filets with olive oil and sprinkle with salt and black pepper. Place the filets on the hot grill, close the lid and cook to just below the desired temperature. Depending on the intensity of your grill, a filet should cook about 8 to 10 minutes per side to reach medium rare, which registers at 120 to 125 degrees on a meat thermometer. There are, however, a number of varying factors in how long to cook the filet: the thickness of the meat, the exact weight of the meat and the heat of the grill. This is why a meat thermometer is helpful.

When you get close to your desired temperature, take the filets off of the grill. Spread the top of each filet with 2 or 3 Tablespoons of Pimiento Cheese. Place the filets back on the grill, close the lid and cook for another 2 to 3 minutes. Serve immediately.

4 filets of beef, 6 to 8 ounces each

2 Tablespoons olive oil

salt and freshly ground black pepper

Pimiento Cheese (see p. 29)

Grilled Tomatoes (see p. 44-45)

Grilled Green Onions (see p. 44-45)

Parslied Potatoes (see p. 38)

Madeira Sauce (see p. 113)

MADEIRA SAUCE

For an ordinary household, this labor intensive reduction sauce is quite a culinary achievement. However, it is well worth the effort when you want an outstanding accompaniment sauce for a fine piece of meat or poultry.

Makes 1 pint.

VEAL STOCK:

Preheat oven to 500 degrees.

Rub the veal bones with a little olive oil. Place the bones on a large baking sheet with raised sides and put it on the top shelf of the 500 degree oven. Roast the bones for 30 to 35 minutes or until a nice dark golden color is obtained. Remove the pan from the oven. Reduce the heat to 450 degrees. Using a rubber spatula or a wooden spoon, smear the bones with the tomato paste. Add the chopped vegetables to the bones and return the pan to the oven. Continue to roast them for another 30 minutes.

Remove the bones and vegetables from the oven. Put them all into a large stockpot. Take a little of the water and deglaze the baking sheet, scraping the bottom to get all of the little bits of browned drippings and vegetables. Add the rest of the water, the chicken broth, bay leaves, peppercorns, thyme, parsley stems and garlic to the stockpot. If the water does not completely cover the bones, add enough to cover.

Slowly bring the stock to a boil, then reduce it to a simmer. It is important not to boil the stock because boiling will make it cloudy. Turn the stock down to a simmer. Skim off the foam that appears on the top and any excessive amounts of fat. Simmer the stock for about 4$1/2$ to 5 hours. It should have a good flavor and color. Strain, pressing all of the juice out of the vegetables.

(continued next page)

VEAL STOCK:

5 pounds veal bones, in small pieces

olive oil

6 ounces tomato paste

1 large yellow onion, roughly chopped

2 carrots, roughly chopped

3 stalks celery, roughly chopped, but with no leaves

white portion of 1 leek, well washed and roughly chopped

12 cups water

4 cups chicken broth

2 bay leaves

6 cracked black peppercorns

8 sprigs of fresh thyme or 1/2 teaspoon dried thyme

10 parsley stems

4 cloves garlic, roughly chopped

Let cool and refrigerate until ready to use.

When stock has been chilled, it is easy to remove the fat from it; the fat will rise to the top and you can lift it off with a spoon. You should have an end product of $1^1/_2$ quarts of degreased veal stock.

SAUCE REDUCTION:

Place the degreased veal stock in a clean saucepan and reduce by one-half over medium heat.

Heat the olive oil in a heavy-bottomed saucepan. Add the onions, garlic, tomatoes, parsley stems and sauté for 1 minute. Add the red wine and Madeira and bring the mixture to a boil. Lower the heat and simmer gently until the liquid is reduced by two-thirds.

Add the reduced veal stock to the rest of the ingredients, and continue to reduce by simmering. You will get a nice, dark color and intensified flavor as the liquid reduces. Reduce the liquid by one-third to approximately $2^1/_2$ cups. Strain the mixture, pressing all of the juices out of the vegetables, then strain again through a fine sieve. Return the sauce to the stove and reduce the volume by another third, skimming off any foam that may come to the top. At this point you may strain once more through cheesecloth or a very fine sieve. Or you may serve the sauce as it is.

Season with salt and white pepper to taste and a splash of Madiera if desired.

NOTE: It is important not to add any salt during the cooking process because salt would concentrate as the liquids are reduced and an oversalted sauce will result.

MADEIRA SAUCE:

$1^1/_2$ **quarts of veal stock from the previous recipe**

1 Tablespoon olive oil

1 cup roughly chopped yellow onions

1 Tablespoon roughly chopped garlic

2 cups roughly chopped tomatoes, juice, seeds and all

$^1/_4$ cup chopped parsley stems

1 cup red wine, of drinking quality

1 cup Madeira wine

salt and white pepper to taste

HERB-SEARED LAMB LOIN WITH NATURAL JUICES

This recipe for loin of lamb is very easy because everything except cooking the loin can be done ahead of time. I recommend serving this with our Buttermilk Mashed Potatoes and Spinach with Roasted Garlic.

2 servings

Trim off all excess fat right down to the membrane covering the loin. With the tip of a knife, remove the loin from the rib bones, reserving the bones and being careful to not cut into the loin. The trimmed, boneless loin should weigh about 12 ounces.

THE MARINADE:

Mix the garlic, ginger, rosemary, sage, thyme, black pepper and olive oil to make a marinade. Rub the boneless loin with the marinade. The loin can be cooked right after it is rubbed or it can sit, covered, in the refrigerator for several hours or overnight.

THE *JUS*:

Heat the olive oil in a heavy-bottomed pan over medium-high heat until the oil is smoking. Add the lamb ribs which have been cut apart and sear them for 3 to 5 minutes, stirring frequently so that they brown evenly. Add the onion, garlic, ginger, carrots, celery, rosemary, bay leaf, peppercorns and parsley stems and continue to brown the mixture for another 3 to 5 minutes. Add the tomato paste and cook for a minute.

Add the chicken broth and deglaze the pan, scraping up all of the browned bits for color and flavor. Gently simmer this mixture for about 8 to 10 minutes to reduce the liquid volume by half, removing any froth that may appear on top. Strain the mixture through a very fine sieve or strainer. Season with salt and freshly

1 loin of lamb, about 1½ pounds

THE MARINADE:

1 teaspoon minced garlic

1 teaspoon peeled, minced ginger

1 teaspoon minced fresh rosemary

1 teaspoon minced fresh sage

1 teaspoon minced fresh thyme

¼ teaspoon freshly ground black pepper

½ teaspoon olive oil

THE *JUS*:

1 teaspoon olive oil

lamb ribs reserved from trimming the loin, cut individually

½ cup roughly chopped yellow onion

1 teaspoon minced garlic

¼ cup roughly chopped ginger

¼ cup roughly chopped carrots

¼ cup roughly chopped celery

1 Tablespoon fresh rosemary

1 bay leaf

4 peppercorns

6 parsley stems

1 Tablespoon plus 1 teaspoon
tomato paste

2 cups chicken broth

salt and freshly ground black
pepper

ground black pepper. The *jus* can be used right after it is made or it can be placed in a storage container, let cool to room temperature, covered and refrigerated.

TO COOK THE LAMB:

Preheat an oven to 350 degrees.

Heat teaspoon of olive oil in a heavy-bottomed pan over medium high heat until the oil is smoking. Gently lay the loin in the oil and sear for 4 to 5 minutes, turning so that all sides are browned evenly. You want to achieve a crisp, seared crust. Place the pan in the 350 degree oven for approximately:

- 5–6 minutes for medium rare
- 8–9 minutes for medium
- 15 minutes for well done

Remove the pan from the oven. Place the loin on a cutting board to rest for a minute. Slice the loin into thin slices and divide between two warmed plates. Drizzle with some of the lamb *jus*. Serve immediately.

CHICKEN AND SAGE HASH WITH POACHED EGGS AND A CRACKED PEPPERCORN HOLLANDAISE

This diverse egg dish is great as a special brunch course or a challenging breakfast for someone that you would like to impress. This dish also makes us curious as to which came first—the chicken or the egg?

4 servings

Preheat oven to 425 degrees.

Toss together 1 Tablespoon of the olive oil, the potatoes, salt and black pepper. Place this mixture on a heavy baking sheet with sides and place it on the top shelf of the 425 degree oven. Bake, uncovered, for 15 to 20 minutes, stirring once, or until the potatoes are a light golden color. Remove and reserve. Heat 2 Tablespoons of the olive oil in a heavy-bottomed skillet over medium high heat. Add the onion, celery, carrot, red peppers and garlic and sauté, stirring, for 2 to 3 minutes, or until the onions are translucent. All of this can be done as much as a day ahead. Remove and cool.

Remove the skin from the chicken thighs. Rub the meat with the teaspoon of olive oil and a little salt and black pepper. Roast the thighs on a baking sheet in the 425 degree oven for 25 to 30 minutes, or until done. Cool to room temperature, remove the meat from the bones and chop it roughly.

When ready to serve, heat the remaining Tablespoon of olive oil in a non-stick frying pan over medium heat. Add the potatoes, vegetables and chopped chicken and toss for 3 to 5 minutes. Add the sage and salt and pepper to taste.

Warm 4 soup bowls and divide the hash among them. Place 2 Poached Eggs on top of each bowl of hash and nap with the Cracked Pepper Hollandaise.

3 Tablespoons plus 1 teaspoon olive oil

3 cups skin-on diced baking potatoes, cut into 1/4-inch dice (about 3 potatoes)

1/4 teaspoon salt

1/2 teaspoon freshly ground black pepper

1/2 cup roughly diced yellow onion

1/2 cup roughly diced celery, no leaves

1/2 cup roughly diced carrot (1 large carrot)

1/2 cup roughly diced red pepper

1 teaspoon minced garlic

1 Tablespoon chopped fresh sage or 1 1/2 teaspoons dried sage

6 chicken thighs, boneless if available (see p. 16)

POACHED EGGS

8 eggs

12 cups water

4 Tablespoons white or cider vinegar

Place the water in a deep, heavy-bottomed pan and heat it to a simmer just below the boiling point. Give the water a swirl with a spatula. Crack the eggs one by one into a cup, then gently slide them into the water.

The eggs will poach with the water temperature at just below a simmer, but with bubbles still breaking to the top occasionally. The cooking times should be:

- 3 minutes for a runny yolk
- 4 minutes for a medium yolk
- 5 minutes for a hard yolk

Remove the eggs from the water with a slotted spoon and serve.

CRACKED PEPPERCORN HOLLANDAISE

Yield: 2 cups

4 egg yolks

1 Tablespoon fresh lemon juice

¹/₄ teaspoon salt

3 dashes Tabasco

3 Tablespoons water

1 pound unsalted butter, melted

1 Tablespoon chopped parsley

1 teaspoon freshly cracked
  pepper

Place the egg yolks, lemon juice, salt, Tabasco and water in a stainless steel bowl, or in the bowl of an electric mixer and mix to combine. Place the bowl over simmering water, double boiler style, but not touching the water. Whisk the yolk mixture vigorously for 3 to 4 minutes until it triples in volume and becomes light in color. It may be necessary to take the bowl off of the stove a couple of times to release the steam which builds up.

When the mixture has tripled in volume and is opaque, remove the bowl from over the simmering water and place it on the counter on a damp cloth to steady it or on the mixer with the whip attachment. Whisking vigorously, pour in the melted butter in a slow, steady stream. The melted butter should be the same temperature as the warm yolk mixture for a tight emulsification. After all of the butter is added, fold in the parsley and cracked pepper. Taste the sauce and adjust the seasoning with salt, cayenne pepper, lemon juice or Tabasco. Serve at once, or you may place the hollandaise in a small glass bowl and keep it in a warm place for about an hour before serving. To successfully be held, the hollandaise should remain at a warm temperature, becoming neither too hot or too cold.

NOTE: When you melt the butter for the hollandaise, you have to do it very slowly. Otherwise the butter will boil and the water in it will cause the golden liquid butter to emulsify with the water and inhibit the butter's ability to thicken. Let the melted butter settle and pour or ladle the golden butter from the top, leaving the water and the milk solids to be discarded. The result is what is known as "clarified butter."

CHICKEN WITH BOW TIE PASTA, ASPARAGUS, COUNTRY HAM AND A CRACKED PEPPER AND PARMESAN CREAM

4 servings

THE PASTA:

Put the water in a stockpot and bring it to boil over high heat. Add the salt just before the pasta is added. Add the pasta, stirring so that it does not stick together. Lower the heat to medium and gently boil the pasta for 8 to 9 minutes or until the pasta is *al dente*. Strain off the water by pouring the pasta into a colander. At this point you may stir the hot pasta right into the sauce and serve immediately.

To do the pasta ahead, place ice cubes in a bowl of cold water and set aside. Drain the pasta. Rinse with cold water and immerse in the ice water to stop the cooking. Drain well, toss with a Tablespoon of olive oil, place in a storage container, cover and store in the refrigerator until ready to use.

THE CRACKED PEPPER AND PARMESAN CREAM:

Heat the olive oil in a heavy-bottomed sauce pan over medium heat. Add the country ham and sauté for 2 minutes. Add the onion, garlic, asparagus and chicken and sauté for another 2 minutes, stirring frequently to prevent the mixture from browning. Add the cream and simmer for 5 minutes. Add the cracked black pepper, Parmesan cheese, 2 Tablespoons of the parsley and the cooked bow tie pasta. Stir to combine and continue stirring until the pasta is warmed. Season with salt and additional black pepper if desired. Spoon into warm soup bowls and serve immediately.

THE PASTA:

1/2 pound bow tie pasta

1/2 gallon water

1 Tablespoon salt

THE CRACKED PARMESAN CREAM:

2 teaspoons olive oil

1/2 cup thin strips of country ham

1/2 cup minced yellow onion

2 teaspoons minced garlic

1 1/2 cups asparagus, cut diagonally in 1/4 inch slices

1 1/4 cups chopped cooked chicken thigh meat (see p. 16)

2 cups heavy cream

1 teaspoon freshly cracked black pepper

1/2 cup freshly grated Parmesan cheese

2 Tablespoons and 1 teaspoon minced parsley

salt to taste

SOUTHERN SWEETS

SOUTHERN SWEETS

Although I get a bit of ribbing about it now, I have to confess that my love of food all began in my younger years when I was growing up in Charleston, West Virginia. I was the second child in a family of three boys and a baby sister, Lucinda. On Lucinda's second Christmas, she was given a small cook set. I immediately took it over, thinking that Lucinda was too little to understand the concept of cooking and that I was the one to get started on such a challenging present.

Even though the set wasn't one of the ones that came with its own oven, it had all of the accessories needed for baking cakes, muffins and cookies. I was quickly off to the kitchen to get going with the recipes which were inclosed. This was the beginning of an on-going hobby. Every year when my Birthday would come around, I would spend the afternoon before in the kitchen with my Mother making cookies to take to my classmates on my special day.

When it came time to do my externship at the Culinary Institute of America, I decided to return home to West Virginia and hone my baking skills. I went to work at the Charleston Marriott and did the midnight baking shift for about nine weeks. This position was a very valuable learning experiences for me and I often refer back to some of the things that I learned there.

In this book, I have shared the recipes for some of our most popular desserts. You can make further use of the parts of these recipes by mixing and matching the sauces and by making the cobbler with the best fruits of the season. You may want to use the pie crust for a favorite filling of your own and there are all sorts of possibilities for the Sweet Biscuit.

One of the things in our desert recipes which you'll notice is our use of "Southern flour." Most commonly available under the labels of White Lily and Martha White, Southern flour is milled from wheat grown specifically for its characteristically low gluten. Exactly the opposite of the high gluten flours desired for chewy pizza crusts and county style breads, a low gluten flour produces a softer, more delicate baked product, perhaps the most noticeable in a biscuit. If a Southern flour is not available exactly when you need it, a combination of 50% cake flour to 50% all purpose flour can be substituted. However, the mail cookware giant, Williams-Sonoma has recently introduced White Lily in their catalogue, so Southern flour is almost as close as your telephone. I suggest that you try some.

Williams-Sonoma
A Catalogue for Cooks
1-800-541-2233

MAGNOLIAS' COBBLER

FILLING:

Combine the berries, sugar, lemon juice, flour and salt, tossing the fruit until it is coated by the other ingredients. Pour the fruit into the baking pan.

TOPPING:

Preheat oven to 350 degrees.

Dice the butter, put it on a plate and place it in the refrigerator to remain cold while you are assembling your other ingredients. Combine the flour, sugar, baking powder and salt and stir to mix well. Add the diced butter and cut it into the flour with either a pastry cutter or 2 forks until the mixture is crumbly. Add the buttermilk a little at a time until the dough starts to come together. However, this dough should not form a ball like a pie dough does. The topping should still be very crumbly, and not sticky. Sprinkle the topping over the filling. It should be about half an inch thick.

Bake the cobbler in the middle of the 350 degree oven for 1 hour or until the topping is a light golden color and the berry filling is bubbling up around the sides. Remove the cobbler from the oven and let it cool for a few minutes. Serve with ice cream or whipped cream. (see p. 138)

NOTE: You may use frozen fruit in the cobbler. However, with frozen fruit you may decrease the sugar by $1/2$ cup.

---

1 9" by 13" baking pan

FILLING

6 cups fresh blue berries

3 cups fresh strawberries

1$1/2$ cups sugar

1 Tablespoon lemon juice

$1/2$ cup Southern flour (see p. 124)

$1/2$ teaspoon salt

TOPPING

6 Tablespoons cold, diced unsalted butter

1$1/2$ cups Southern flour

$1/2$ cup sugar

$1/2$ teaspoon non-alum baking powder (see p. 31)

$1/2$ teaspoon salt

$1/4$ cup plus 1 Tablespoon buttermilk

MAGNOLIAS' BAKED CREAMS WITH ORANGE CUSTARD SAUCE

4 cups milk

1¹/₂ cups sugar

¹/₂ vanilla bean, slit down one side, or 1 teaspoon pure vanilla extract

rind of 1 orange, roughly chopped

6 whole eggs

4 egg yolks

fresh fruit to garnish

This is the custard lover's custard. It leaves out the caramelized sugar syrup which classically accompanied these creams. We prefer the Orange Custard Sauce. The milk in the recipe is infused with fresh orange peel so that it also has a subtle orange flavor.

Makes 8 Baked Creams

Preheat oven to 300 degrees. You will need 8 six ounce ramekins or heat-proof custard cups and a roasting pan large enough to hold them.

Take the outer layer of the rind off of an orange with either a vegetable peeler or a zester. You do not want any of the white under layer as it is bitter.

Place the milk, 3/4 cup of the sugar, the vanilla bean and orange rind in a heavy-bottomed saucepan over medium heat. Slowly bring the mixture to a boil. Remove the mixture from the heat and strain. Scrape the inside of the vanilla bean, putting the seeds back into the hot milk. Discard the rind of the vanilla bean and the orange rind.

In a separate bowl, beat together the eggs, egg yolks and the remaining sugar until combined. Slowly stream the warm milk mixture in 1 cup at a time, whisking continuously. When half of the milk is incorporated into the egg mixture, slowly pour the mixture back into the pan of hot milk, whisking continuously.

Divide the mixture into the eight ramekins and sit them in the roasting pan. Place the pan on the middle shelf of the 300 degree oven. Pull the shelf out and add enough hot water to the pan to come halfway up the sides of the ramekins, making sure, however, not to get any water into the creams. This "water bath" deflects the direct heat which would cook the outside of the creams before the insides finish cooking. Bake the creams at 300 degrees for approximately 1 hour and 40 minutes or until the

creams are firm. A knife inserted into the center of one of the creams should come out without any milky liquid on it.

Chill the creams for 4 hours or overnight. Gently run a knife around the inside edges of the ramekins. Unmold the creams on individual dessert plates. Serve with Orange Custard Sauce, and garnish with fresh fruit.

ORANGE CUSTARD SAUCE

You'll find many ways to use this sauce. It goes especially well with dense, rich chocolate desserts.

Makes 2 cups

rind of ¹/₂ orange

¹/₂ cup sugar

2 cups heavy cream

¹/₄ vanilla bean, split down one side, or 1 teaspoon pure vanilla extract

4 egg yolks

Take the outer orange layer of the rind off of an orange with either a vegetable peeler or a zester. You do not want any of the white under layer as it is bitter tasting.

Place ¹/₄ cup of the sugar, the whipping cream, the orange rind and the vanilla bean in a heavy-bottomed saucepan and stir over medium heat to dissolve the sugar. Slowly bring the cream to a low boil, stirring to prevent scorching.

In a separate bowl, beat the egg yolks with the remaining sugar until combined. Slowly stream in 1 cup of the hot cream. When half of the cream is incorporated into the yolks, slowly pour the mixture back into the pan of hot cream, whisking continuously. Place the pan over low heat and, stirring constantly with a wooden spoon, cook the custard until it is thick enough to coat the back of the spoon. Remove the pan from the heat and strain the custard into a glass or crockery storage container. Scrape the inside of the vanilla bean, putting the seeds into the custard. Discard the rind of the bean itself and the orange rind. Let the custard cool at room temperature for 15 minutes, stirring occasionally. Strain the custard into a storage container with a lid and place in the refrigerator. When the custard is cold, cover it. Serve cold. Orange Custard will keep in the refrigerator for 2-3 days.

WARM CREAM CHEESE BROWNIES WITH VANILLA BEAN ICE CREAM, CHOCOLATE AND CARAMEL SAUCE

Days before finalizing our first dessert menu at Magnolias, I sampled one of these at Nancy Smith's house. It was typical of her simple ideas and warm hospitality. The brownies are great alone, but we dress them up with ice cream, chocolate and caramel sauces. Cream Cheese Brownies won't be forgotten in the Barickman family because they also provided a perfect surprise hiding place for my wife's engagement ring.

Makes 24 brownies

Beat the cream cheese, butter and sugar until well blended. Add the eggs one at a time, beating well and scraping down the sides of the bowl at least once. Beat in the vanilla. Fold in the flour and chips and set aside.

Preheat oven to 325 degrees. Using a vegetable shortening, grease the 9" x 13" pan, line it with foil and grease the foil.

Melt the chocolate and butter in a double boiler or over very low heat. Remove from the heat and cool to room temperature. Beat the eggs, gradually adding the sugar, until the eggs are thick and light in color. Blend in the cooled chocolate mixture. Add the vanilla and combine well.

Combine the flour, baking powder and salt. Fold it into the chocolate mixture. Fold in the chocolate chips. Reserve 2 cups of this chocolate batter. Spoon the rest into the greased baking pan. Spread the cream cheese batter on top of this chocolate batter. Spoon the reserved chocolate batter on top. To achieve a marbled effect and the binding of the two layers, swirl them with a knife or icing spatula.

Bake the brownies in the 325 degree oven for 35 to 40 minutes or until a cake tester comes out clean. The edges of the brownies will have puffed, but the center will still be fairly soft. The center

1 9" x 13" pan

CREAM CHEESE BATTER:

6 ounces cream cheese, room temperature

4 Tablespoons unsalted butter, room temperature

1/2 cup sugar

2 large eggs

1 teaspoon pure vanilla extract

2 Tablespoons all purpose flour

1/2 cup semi-sweet chocolate chips

CHOCOLATE BATTER:

4 ounces unsweetened chocolate

4 ounces semi-sweet chocolate

6 Tablespoons unsalted butter

4 large eggs

1 1/2 cups sugar

2 teaspoons pure vanilla extract

1 teaspoon non-alum baking powder (see p. 31)

1 teaspoon salt

1 cup semi-sweet chocolate chips

1 cup all-purpose flour

will firm up, however, because it will continue to cook even after the pan is removed from the oven. Cool the brownies in the pan before cutting. They should be very rich and moist.

CHOCOLATE SAUCE

1 cup heavy cream

1/2 pound semi-sweet chocolate

It doesn't matter whether you use chopped blocks of chocolate or chocolate chips as long as you use a good quality chocolate, preferably on the dark side.

Makes $1^3/4$ cups

Heat the cream to a boil in a heavy-bottomed sauce pan over medium heat. Place the chocolate in a mixing bowl and add the boiling cream, whisking continuously until the chocolate has melted and the sauce is smooth. Use at once or cool to room temperature, pour into a storage container and refrigerate. The sauce should keep for several weeks in the refrigerator.

CARAMEL SAUCE

8 Tablespoons unsalted butter

1 cup light brown sugar

1/2 cup heavy cream

1/2 teaspoon pure vanilla extract

dash of salt

Makes $1^1/2$ cups.

Melt the butter and sugar in a heavy-bottomed saucepan and stir over medium heat until the sugar is completely dissolved and the mixture is thick and bubbly. Slowly add the cream in small amounts, stirring constantly. Add the vanilla and salt and bring the mixture to a boil, stirring. Remove the caramel from the heat. Use at once or cool to room temperature, pour into a storage container with a lid and refrigerate. The caramel should keep in the refrigerator for several weeks.

NOTE: Both the chocolate and the caramel sauces can be rewarmed by stirring them over simmering water in a double boiler or microwaving them very gently.

PIE CRUST

Chilling the pie crust dough between steps as indicated allows the gluten to relax and keeps the butter and shortening cold. This helps to ensure a tender crust and to keep the sides from shrinking and slipping down. Patting the dough out into thin disks helps to eliminate the difficulty of rolling it out evenly.

Makes 2 10" crusts

Dice the butter. Measure the shortening. Put the butter and the shortening on a plate and place it in the refrigerator to firm the shortening and keep the butter cold while you are assembling the other ingredients.

Combine the flour, salt and sugar. Add the diced butter and shortening. Cut them into the flour with either a pie cutter or 2 forks until butter is completely cut in and is no bigger than small peas. Slowly add the ice water, lightly combining the ingredients until they come together to form a ball. Pat the dough into 2 round, thin flat disks, eliminating any creases and smoothing the edges. Wrap the disks in plastic wrap and refrigerate for a least an hour or until firm.

When you are ready to make the pie crusts, roll the dough out one piece at a time on a lightly floured surface. Roll it into an approximately 12 inch circle which is about $1/8$-inch thick, giving the dough quarter inch turns as you are rolling it so that the thickness remains uniform. Brush off any excess flour. Roll the dough over your rolling pin and lay it into pie tin. Pat it in to fit the tin. Push the side crust up a little and trim off the overhanging outside crust with the back edge of a knife. Crimp the edges of the crust with 2 fingers and a thumb.

Put the pie crust into the refrigerator to let it chill for at least an hour. When ready to bake, fill the crusts with the desired filling and bake as directed.

15 Tablespoons cold unsalted butter

4 Tablespoons Crisco

3 cups Southern flour (see p. 124)

1 teaspoon salt

1 teaspoon sugar

$2/3$ cup ice water

SWEET POTATO PIE WITH WHITE CHOCOLATE AND BOURBON SAUCE

This dessert is the result of assistant pastry chef Cherette Jupiter's baking skills and flavor combinations. Traditionally a very Southern dessert, this Sweet Potato Pie has a unique addition of white chocolate chunks inside and looks very, very uptown with a crown of white chocolate curls.

Makes 1 pie.

Preheat oven to 400 degrees.

Wash, dry and rub the sweet potatoes with cooking oil. Pierce each potato once or twice with a fork to let the interior steam escape. Bake in the 400 degree oven for 45 minutes to an hour, or until the potatoes are soft. Cool the potatoes until you are able to handle them, then peel them.

Reduce the oven heat to 350 degrees.

Place a heavy baking sheet on the bottom rack of the oven 5 minutes before putting the pie in the oven. This will provide extra heat to help brown the bottom crust.

Place the peeled potatoes in bowl of an electric mixer, add the sugar and mix with the flat paddle to mash until smooth. Scrape the sides and bottom of the bowl at least 2 times while mixing. Add the egg and blend in. Add the milk, cinnamon, nutmeg and vanilla. Mix well to combine. Fold in the white chocolate chunks.

Pour the sweet potato filling into the pie shell. Spread evenly. Sprinkle the top with brown sugar if desired. Place the pie on the baking sheet on the bottom shelf of the 350 degree oven. Bake the pie for 20 minutes. Move the pan to the middle shelf and continue to bake for 30 to 40 minutes, or until the crust is golden.

(continued on next page)

1 10" pie pan

1 pie crust (see p. 131)

2½ cups baked and peeled sweet potatoes (about 3 pounds raw)

vegetable cooking oil

1¼ cups light brown sugar

1 egg

¼ cup whole milk

½ teaspoon ground cinnamon

¼ teaspoon ground nutmeg

1 Tablespoon pure vanilla

1 cup chunks or pieces of white chocolate (about 7 ounces)

3 Tablespoons light brown sugar (optional)

133

Move the pan to the middle shelf and continue to bake for 30 to 40 minutes, or until crust is golden and the filling is slightly puffed. Remove the pie from the oven and let cool to room temperature before slicing.

NOTE: Adding the sugar on the top is optional. It adds a crispy, sugary topping, but it also increases the sweetness of the pie. At different times of the year, the sugar content of the sweet potato varies. If the potatoes are especially sweet, you may not want to add the topping. Taste the potatoes after they are baked to make your determination.

BOURBON SAUCE

2 sticks unsalted butter, diced

1 cup and 2 Tablespoons firmly packed dark brown sugar

¹/₂ cup heavy cream

¹/₄ cup Bourbon

Makes 2 cups

Melt the butter and sugar in a heavy-bottomed saucepan over medium heat, whisking continuously for 5 to 10 minutes or until the butter melts and the sugar is completely dissolved.

Slowly whisk in the cream and then the Bourbon. Use at once or cool to room temperature, pour into a storage container and refrigerate. The sauce should keep for a week in the refrigerator.

To rewarm the sauce, stir it over simmering water in a double boiler or over very low heat. If the heat is too high, the sauce may separate.

CHOCOLATE CHIP BOURBON PECAN PIE

This old favorite makes a great addition to a winter dinner menu. In the fall, the plump pecans have just come off of the trees and they bake up crisp. The chocolate and the bourbon add to the decadence.

1 10" pie pan

Makes 1 pie

Preheat oven to 350 degrees.

Place a heavy baking sheet on the bottom rack of the oven for 5 minutes before putting the pie in the oven. This will provide extra heat to help brown the bottom crust.

Place the eggs, sugar, corn syrup, vanilla and Bourbon in a bowl and mix. Scrape the sides and bottom of the bowl at least 2 times while mixing. Add the warm butter. Mix well. Combine the pecans and chocolate chips and sprinkle them on the bottom of the pie shell. Pour the filling over the nuts and chips.

Place the pie on the baking sheet on the bottom shelf of the 350 degree oven and bake it for 30 minutes. Move the pie to the middle shelf and continue to bake it for another 15 to 20 minutes. The edges of the filling will rise, but the middle will still be a little bouncy. However, the pie will continue to bake after it is removed from the oven. To set up and have it firm enough to slice, give the pie 2 to 3 hours of cooling at room temperature, or a half hour of cooling at room temperature and an hour in the refrigerator.

You may serve the pie as is or add Vanilla Ice Cream or Bourbon Sauce.

1 10 " pie crust (see p. 131)

4 large eggs, room temperature

$\frac{1}{2}$ cup plus 2 Tablespoons sugar

1$\frac{1}{2}$ cups dark corn syrup

1 Tablespoon pure vanilla extract

2 Tablespoons bourbon

6 Tablespoons unsalted butter, melted and kept warm

1$\frac{1}{2}$ cups chopped pecans

$\frac{3}{4}$ cup semi-sweet chocolate chips

BISCUITS:

7 Tablespoons cold, diced unsalted butter

2 cups and 2 Tablespoons Southern flour (see p. 124)

3 Tablespoons sugar

1 Tablespoon non-alum baking powder (see p. 31)

3/4 teaspoon salt

3 ounces buttermilk

2 Tablespoons heavy cream to brush tops

2 Tablespoons sugar for tops

FILLING:

2 pints of strawberries, washed, stemmed and sliced

2 Tablespoons sugar

WHIPPED CREAM:

2 cups whipping cream

3 Tablespoons sugar

1/2 teaspoon pure vanilla extract

SWEET BISCUIT WITH FRESH STRAWBERRIES AND WHIPPED CREAM

At Magnolias, we serve the Sweet Biscuits with strawberries and whipped cream. The Orange Custard Sauce also works well with the biscuit, served with seasonal fresh fruit.

Makes 8 2¹/₂-inch biscuits

Preheat oven to 375 degrees.

Dice the butter, put it on a plate and put it back into the refrigerator to remain cold while you are assembling the other ingredients. Combine the flour, sugar, baking powder and salt. Add the diced butter and cut it into the flour with either a pastry cutter or 2 forks until the mixture is crumbly.

Add the buttermilk a little at a time until the dough comes together and forms a ball. Place it on a floured work service, sprinkle it with flour and pat it out into a one-inch high circle. Cut the biscuits with a 2¹/₂-inch cutter and place them on a heavy baking pan. Brush the tops of the biscuits with the heavy cream, then sprinkle with the 2 Tablespoons of sugar.

Place the pan on the middle shelf of the 375 degree oven and bake for 15 to 20 minutes. Check the center of one biscuit and if it isn't baked through, continue to bake for another 5 to 8 minutes. If the outside of the biscuits becomes too brown and the center is still doughy, loosely cover the biscuits with aluminum foil. Remove the biscuits from the oven and let cool to room temperature.

When you are ready to serve the biscuits, toss the sliced strawberries with the sugar and let them sit for 5 minutes before plating them. The combination of sugar and the juices from the berries will produce a nice syrup.

Keep your whipping cream very cold. Combine it with the 2 Tablespoons sugar and the vanilla. Place the bowl over a large bowl filled with ice cubes and whip the cream vigorously for 3 to 5 minutes or until soft peaks are obtained.

To serve: split the biscuits and place the bottom half on each plate. Spoon the strawberries over the bottom halves, add a dollop of whipped cream and replace the tops. Serve immediately.

BENNE SEED BISCUITS

For the Benne Seed Biscuit variation that we served at The James Beard House in 1994, we made the dessert with apples sautéed in butter and brown sugar, a dried cherry and cranberry chutney and a caramel sauce.

To make the biscuits, toast $1/4$ cup plus 1 Tablespoon of benne seeds on a sheet pan in a 350 degree oven for 15 to 20 minutes until they are golden brown and have a toasted aroma, watching and stirring occasionally to make sure that they don't burn. Add the $1/4$ cup toasted benne seeds to the biscuits' dry ingredients and make the biscuits as directed above. Brush the tops of the biscuits with cream, sprinkle the remaining Tablespoon of benne seeds on top, then sprinkle with sugar. Bake as directed above.

In Charleston, plain sesame seeds have always been called benne seeds. They are usually available in bulk at a health food store at a much lower price than in a spice bottle at the grocery store.

139

INDEX

CREDITS

Brittain's of Charleston
180 King Street
Charleston, South Carolina 29401
For the china on p. 14, 52, 66, 71, 76,
93, 99, 107, 113, 119, 126, 132, 137

By The Yard
4 Avondale Avenue
Charleston, South Carolina 29407
For fabrics from their fine selection.

The Charleston Museum
360 Meeting Street
Charleston, South Carolina 29403
For use of the herb garden of the
Heyward-Washington House, p. 34–35

Rod Goebel
Rod Goebel Gallery
110 Paseo del Pueblo Norte
Taos, New Mexico 87571
For oil paintings on p. ii, vii, 139

Magnolias commissioned celebrated artist
Rod Goebel (1946–1993) to create the art work
exhibited throughout the restaurant.